Book Three Of The "Heaven Now" Series

Jesus Has Come In The Flesh

Propiv Press
Lancaster Pennsylvania, USA

Jesus Has Come In The Flesh

By Jonathan Brenneman

Jesus Has Come In The Flesh

Copyright © 2016 by Jonathan Brenneman. All rights reserved. This book is protected by the copyright laws of the United States of America. This book may not be copied or reprinted for commercial gain or profit. The use of short quotations or occasional page copying for personal or group study is permitted and encouraged. Permission will be granted upon request.

General Editor Arnolda M. Brenneman
Contributing Editor John Lee

Propiv Press, Lancaster, Pennsylvania, USA

ISBN-13: 978-1537649061
ISBN-10: 153764906X

Printed in the United States of America.

Unless otherwise indicated, scripture quotations are taken from the New Revised Standard Version Bible, copyright © 1989 the Division of Christian Education of the National Council of the Churches of Christ in the United States of America. Used by permission. All rights reserved.

Scripture quotations marked AMP are taken from the Amplified® Bible Copyright © 2015 by The Lockman Foundation. Used by permission. Scripture quotations marked KJV are taken from the 1769 King James Version of the Holy Bible, Public Domain. Scripture quotations marked NIV are taken from THE HOLY BIBLE, NEW INTERNATIONAL VERSION®, NIV® Copyright © 1973, 1978, 1984, 2011 by Biblica, Inc.® Used by permission. All rights reserved worldwide. Scripture quotations marked RSV are taken from the Revised Standard Version, copyright ©1962 by the World Publishing Company. All rights reserved. Scripture quotations marked YLT are taken from Young's Literal Translation of the Holy Bible by J. N. Young, 1862, 1898, Public Domain. Scripture quotations marked NKJV are taken from the New King James Version®. Copyright © 1982 by Thomas Nelson. Used by permission. All rights reserved. Scripture quotations noted CEB are taken from the Common English Bible, copyright 2011. Used by permission. All rights reserved. Scripture quotations marked JUB are taken from The Jubilee Bible (from the Scriptures of the Reformation) edited by Russel M. Stendal, Copyright © 2000,2001,2010

This book is not intended as a substitute for the medical advice of physicians. The reader should regularly consult a physician in matters relating to his/her health and particularly with respect to any symptoms that may require diagnosis or medical attention.

Dedication

I dedicate this work to the body of Christ: to all Christians, in whose flesh the Spirit of Jesus dwells.

Book Three in the "Heaven Now" trilogy

Jesus Has Come In The Flesh

Table of Contents

Introduction xiii
1. Antichrists 1
   Who Is "The Antichrist?" 1
   Isn't "Antichrist" A Strong Word? 4
   Can A Christian Be Influenced By An Antichrist Spirit? 5
2. The Incarnation Shows The Body Is Holy 7
   The Sanctity Of The Body 7
   Physical Salvation 7
   Sharing Our Faith With Confidence 16
   An Antichrist Spirit Teaches Salvation Is For The Spirit And Soul, Not The Body 16
3. Gnosticism, Sex, And The Church 19
   Gnostic Influence In The Church 19
   Glorify God With Your Body — Because Jesus Has Come In Your Flesh 22
4. An Antichrist Spirit Promotes Sexual Immorality And Violence 25
   Counterfeits 25
   The Body-Soul-Spirit Connection And Sexuality 26
   Fatherlessness 35
   STDs/STIs 40
   Violence And Substance Abuse 43

Loss Of Natural Affection 45

5. Re-Sensitization And Undoing The Works Of The Devil 53

The Incarnation Undoes The Works Of The Devil 53

Healing And Spiritual Warfare 54

An Infection Under The Tongue 55

Delivered From Alcoholism When She Realized God Healed Her! 56

Meeting Physical Needs 58

6. The Incarnation Means We Can Touch God 63

The Word We Have Touched With Our Hands 63

God Is With Us! 65

Giving People A Sign 67

Offer Your Body To The Lord 68

7. Why Did Jesus Have To Come As A Man? 71

Man's Authority 71

Jesus Demonstrated The Authority God Gave Man By Coming As A Man 77

The Antichrist Spirit Denies The Authority God Gave To Man 78

What Is Satan Afraid Of? 80

When Not To Cry Out To God 80

An Antichrist Spirit Says God Controls Everything 82

8. We Can Know God's Will Because Jesus Came In The Flesh
 87

The Mystery Of God's Will Revealed In Christ 87

An Antichrist Spirit Says God's Will Is A Mystery 91

An Antichrist Spirit Teaches People To View God Through Anything But Jesus 91

9. The Antichrist Spirit Resists The Revelation Of Christ 97

Avoiding Jesus 97

"The Power Of Faith Is Amazing" 97
"You Have Such An Amazing Spiritual Gift!" 99
"What Church Do You Go To?" 100
Talk About Jesus! 101
An Antichrist Spirit Says You Need Special Knowledge Because Jesus Isn't Enough 101

10. I Can Do The Things Jesus Did, Because Jesus Has Come In My Flesh 107

Jesus' Commission To His Disciples Extended to Us! 107
Jesus Became Like Us In Every Way 108
If You Believe You Will See The Glory Of God 109
Frustration And Making Healing Too Complicated 114
Meeting Dan Mohler 117
Why Did Jesus Only Heal A Few People At Nazareth? Why Did He Put Everyone Out Before Raising A Girl From The Dead? 119
What Happened When I Simplified Things? 121
Nothing That Didn't Limit Jesus Should Limit Us 125

11. The Antichrist Spirit Denies Christ Lives In You 127

You've Already Overcome All Antichrists, If Jesus Lives In You! 127
Confronting Excruciating Pain And Much More 128
Shut Up You Lying Spirit! 128
Dealing With Spiritual Opposition To The Message 130
Be As Gracious As Possible, But Be Assertive! 131
Dealing With Disruptive Prayers 132
What Was Happening? 134

12. God's Dwelling Place 135

An Anti-Christ Spirit Says A Building Is God's House But Denies Your Body Is His Temple 135

Keep Swinging The Hammer! 140
Walking In The Anointing 141
Appendix: Jesus Come in the Flesh Vs. The Lies of an Antichrist Spirit 143
About The Author 147
Contact 149
Also By Jonathan Brenneman 150

Introduction

Jesus Has Come In The Flesh is the third book in the *Heaven Now* series. Like the first two books, it presents scriptural truths that have resulted in miracles and demonstrations of God's nature and of his power, as I came to understand them.

Many times, as these scriptures came together in my mind, God's glory overwhelmed me until I wept. Jesus has become more real to me than ever before, and I have come to love him all the more.

My main purpose in writing this book wasn't to talk about physical healing, However, *Jesus Has Come In The Flesh* focuses a lot on physical healing, because many implications of the incarnation relate directly to physical healing.

More than anything, I want the reader to experience God's glory and love, which are revealed through the truth that Jesus came in the flesh. In *I Will Awaken The Dawn,* I recounted when my eyes were opened and God's goodness became so real to me that my body vibrated and I was physically healed.

In the same way, I expect many reading this to be physically healed by the manifestation of God's glory as you meditate on the scriptural truths presented. The demonstration of the anointing through your life will increase as you recognize the lies of an antichrist spirit and embrace the truth that Jesus has come in the flesh.

1. Antichrists
Who Is "The Antichrist?"

What have you heard about *"the antichrist?"* Have you heard that *"the antichrist"* might possibly be Bill Gates, the pope, the president of the United States, or someone else?

Martin Luther and the leaders of the Protestant Reformation accused the pope of being the antichrist. Since then, whole books have been written accusing various world-leaders of being the antichrist. Hundreds and thousands of suspected *"antichrists"* have come and gone over the last several hundred years.

Many people may be surprised to learn the word *"antichrist"* doesn't even appear in the book of Revelation. Neither does it appear in the book of Daniel or any of the other prophetic books. We only find it in the epistles of First and Second John.

We've heard much wild speculation around the term *"antichrist."* However, we've had little teaching on what the Bible actually says about antichrists. Only four verses in the entire Bible use this term. Let's look at them. The first scriptural passage mentioning the antichrist is in First John chapter 2:

1 John 2:18-23 (NKJV) Little children, it is the last hour; and as you have heard that the Antichrist is coming, even now many antichrists have come, by which we know that it is the last hour. They went out from us, but they were not of us; for if they had been of us, they would have continued with us; but they went out that they might be made manifest, that none of them were of us.

Jesus Has Come In The Flesh

But you have an anointing from the Holy One, and you know all things. I have not written to you because you do not know the truth, but because you know it, and that no lie is of the truth.

Who is a liar but he who denies that Jesus is the Christ? He is antichrist who denies the Father and the Son. Whoever denies the Son does not have the Father either; he who acknowledges the Son has the Father also.

Notice what the apostle John said. At the time he was writing there were already *"many antichrists."* Who was antichrist? Not a super-sensationalized, evil world leader. Anybody who denied Jesus was the Christ, was antichrist!

The word *"Christ"* literally means *"anointed one."* Jesus is God's anointed one. An antichrist spirit is anti-anointing. It opposes the anointing.

The word *"Christian"* literally means *"little Christ"* or *"little anointed one."* The apostle John contrasts antichrists with Christians, saying *"you have an anointing from the Holy One."* We know the truth because we have an anointing from God. What is anointing? It is the Spirit of God in man, empowering us to do God's will.

We must recognize the lies of an antichrist spirit so we can break agreement with them. When we stop agreeing with lies which oppose the anointing God has given us, we'll demonstrate heaven's reality abundantly through our lives.

John wrote again in First John 4 and in Second John about the *"spirit of antichrist."* How can we recognize this spirit?

1 John 4:1-6 (RSV) Beloved, do not believe every spirit, but test the spirits to see whether they are of God; for many false prophets have gone out into the world. By this you know the Spirit of God: every spirit which confesses that Jesus Christ has come in the flesh is of God, and every spirit which does not confess Jesus is not of God.

This is the spirit of antichrist, of which you heard that it was coming, and now it is in the world already. Little

1. Antichrists

children, you are of God, and have overcome them; for he who is in you is greater than he who is in the world.

They are of the world, therefore what they say is of the world, and the world listens to them. We are of God. Whoever knows God listens to us, and he who is not of God does not listen to us. By this we know the spirit of truth and the spirit of error.

2 John 1:7 (KJV) For many deceivers are entered into the world, who confess not that Jesus Christ is come in the flesh. This is a deceiver and an antichrist.

"Jesus came in the flesh" means Jesus came in a human body. The theological term is *"the incarnation."* I stick to simple language as much as possible in this book, but I will often use the term *"incarnation"* because it's a single word which sums up the truth that Jesus came in the flesh.

I should note here that the Bible uses the word *"flesh"* in various ways, some of which are obviously positive and some which may seem negative. However, we shouldn't misunderstand any part of scripture as saying the body is bad. God himself said it was *"very good"* when he created it.[1] The body is good, but we are to control it, not live under its control. We are to be masters of our bodies, not servants. The fruit of the Spirit is self-control.[2]

First John tells us how we can test the spirits. Every spirit that acknowledges the incarnation is from God. It seems all truth, in some way, relates to the fact that Jesus has come in the flesh. *Any* spirit that denies Jesus has come in the flesh is antichrist. Look at the words of Christ.

Luke 11:23 Whoever is not with me is against me, and whoever does not gather with me scatters.

---

[1] Genesis 1:31
[2] Galatians 5:32

Jesus Has Come In The Flesh

There's no middle ground here. Either the spirit acknowledges Jesus has come in the flesh, and is of God, or it denies the incarnation, and is not of God. *Every* spirit that's not of God is an antichrist spirit. *Every* spirit that's not of God denies that Jesus has come in the flesh.

Some early Church fathers, such as Irenaeus, seemed to think that all heresies were Gnosticism at root, and thus that any heretic was in a sense a Gnostic.[3]

I agree! In historical context, John addressed the teachings of the Gnostics. This was a sect which denied the incarnation. The antichrists John spoke of were teachers of his time. However, John's teaching is just as applicable today as it was then. Any spirit which is not of God is antichrist, and we can test the spirits by understanding the truth that Jesus has come in the flesh.

Notice John wrote that we who are of God have *already overcome* all antichrists. This is what scripture says, and it is absolutely contrary to the fantastical teachings we have heard of an antichrist figure overcoming Christians and taking over the world. We have overcome antichrist because Christ, the Anointed One, lives in us.

We can discern if spirits are of God by understanding that Christ has come in the flesh. We can also discern between truth and error. We can test any spirit and any teaching by this truth.

Isn't "Antichrist" A Strong Word?

Notice that the Apostle John talked about people who were antichrists, and spirits that were antichrist. He also hinted at teaching that was antichrist.

When we understand the scriptural implications of the incarnation, we will recognize teaching that's antichrist. Antichrist teaching denies everything the incarnation implies.

---

[3]Online. https://en.wikipedia.org/wiki/Christian_Gnosticism

1. Antichrists

Antichrist teaching is in opposition to the anointing. Its influence hinders Christians from demonstrating God's nature and his power through their lives.

I'm addressing some controversial issues. I realize the word *"antichrist,"* which has been sensationalized, has the potential to be upsetting! Yet I don't use the word *"antichrist"* to intentionally stir up strife or controversy. I simply use it in its proper context as a biblical term for teaching which is not from God.

By calling certain doctrines and beliefs *"antichrist,"* I do not label all Christians influenced by these doctrines as *"antichrists."* I don't imply that those taught wrongly aren't genuinely saved. I'm saying that these beliefs are not in agreement with the truth that Jesus came in the flesh. These doctrines have hindered the demonstration of the anointing through the body of Christ, the church.

We can test any false religious teaching by understanding the significance of the incarnation. One the other hand, when I read the Bible, I constantly read *"Jesus has come in the flesh"* between the lines. As we proceed, you will see how several passages of scripture relate to the incarnation. If I wanted to write a really long book, I could go through chapter after chapter of scripture and point out how its content is summarized in the incarnation. The word of God is bursting with all the incarnation embodies.

Can A Christian Be Influenced By An Antichrist Spirit?

I think we all recognize that Christians can be influenced by spirits or beliefs that aren't of God. The influence of an ungodly belief doesn't mean a person isn't born again. However, such beliefs hinder our effectiveness and the ability to fully experience all God has for us.

The Holy Spirit opened my eyes to see the scriptural implications of Jesus coming in the flesh. When I understood the truths implied by the incarnation, I also recognized how erroneous beliefs I had once held came from a spirit denying

Jesus come in the flesh. I saw how such beliefs had crippled me for years, keeping me in a place of frustration and powerlessness by opposing the anointing God has given me.

When I began to break free from the influence of antichrist teachings, I started to see the miracles described by scripture happening through my own hands. I came to understand the nature and goodness of Jesus in a much greater way than I ever had before.

Present Access To Heaven describes how Satan would love for us to mentally acknowledge the truths that Jesus died for our sins and rose from the dead, but get us to doubt the practical implications of these truths. Satan would love for our hearts to become inoculated to the glory and power of the gospel message, so he encourages us to embrace a weakened version of it.

In the same way, Christians can acknowledge Christ has come in the flesh, but think and act as if he hasn't. Such Christians are not antichrists, but have been influenced by the teaching of an antichrist spirit.

We have all, at one time or another, embraced some of the lies of an antichrist spirit. As we come to better understand the incarnation, we will recognize these lies and break agreement with them. This, in turn, will free us from a lot of frustration!

The manifestation of God's anointing through my life has increased as I've come to understand these scriptural truths. I write to help people who, as I did, feel frustrated with seeing little manifestation of God's power through their lives. I share the scriptural truths that have helped me the most, to encourage others.

2. The Incarnation Shows The Body Is Holy

The Sanctity Of The Body

In the last chapter, we mentioned that the Apostle John especially addressed the Gnostic teaching of his day. Why did the Gnostics deny Jesus' coming in the flesh?

The Gnostics believed the spirit was holy and pure, but the physical body was evil. If that were true, a holy God could never have come to earth in an evil, human body.

The fact Jesus came in the flesh — in a physical, human body — demonstrates the body's sanctity. The physical body isn't evil, but is a gift from God. Gnosticism taught we must be redeemed from the material world. Christianity teaches that God redeems the material world.

An antichrist spirit denies the value and sanctity of the physical body, calling it evil. As the Gnostics did, it also denies the sanctity of the physical realm in general.

This is one of the ways we can test the spirits to see whether they are from God. If a spirit makes the physical realm out to be either evil or unimportant, it's not from God. It is antichrist. Any spirit or teaching that denies the sanctity of the human body is antichrist in nature.

Physical Salvation

In *Present Access To Heaven*, we look at the Greek word *"sozo,"* translated *"saved"* in commonly quoted verses like Ephesians 2:8. We see that the same word is used repeatedly in the gospels in reference to physical healing. To refresh your memory, here are two examples of the word *"sozo."* The translation of *"sozo"* is underlined.

Jesus Has Come In The Flesh

Ephesians 2:8-9 (NIV) For it is by grace you have been <u>saved</u>, through faith—and this is not from yourselves, it is the gift of God—not by works, so that no one can boast.

Mark 6:56 (NIV) And wherever he went—into villages, towns or countryside—they placed the sick in the marketplaces. They begged him to let them touch even the edge of his cloak, and all who touched it were <u>healed</u>.

The scriptural promises of salvation apply to physical healing as well as to forgiveness of sins and spiritual regeneration. We see the same thing throughout scripture. Some of it is lost in our English translations, as in the different English translations of the same Greek word, *"sozo."* Jesus came to save the whole person — body, soul, and spirit.

Hebrews 7:25 (NIV) Therefore he is able to save completely those who come to God through him

Ephesians 5:23 (YLT) ... the husband is head of the wife, as also the Christ [is] head of the assembly, and he is saviour of the body

1 Thessalonians 5:23 May the God of peace himself sanctify you entirely; and may your spirit and soul and body be kept sound and blameless at the coming of our Lord Jesus Christ.

You aren't just a spirit. Your body is holy and valuable to God. Jesus didn't just come spiritually. He came in a physical, human body. Jesus didn't just suffer spiritually to redeem your spirit. He suffered physically to redeem your body. He came in the flesh and suffered in the flesh.

Romans 8:3 For God has done what the law, weakened by the flesh, could not do: by sending his own Son in the likeness of sinful flesh, and to deal with sin, he condemned sin in the flesh

2 The Incarnation Shows The Body Is Holy

Romans 8:3 (CEB) God has done what was impossible for the Law, since it was weak because of selfishness. God condemned sin in the body by sending his own Son to deal with sin in the same body as humans, who are controlled by sin.

The preacher John G. Lake interpreted *"sin in the flesh"* as disease.[4] When I first read his interpretation, this was a new thought for me. However, it makes a lot of sense in the light of modern science. The neurologist Dr. Carolyn Leaf states that research shows 87-95% of disease is primarily caused by toxic thinking. In her book *Who Switched off my Brain?,*[5] she explains in technical and scientific terms how thoughts affect the body through the endocrine and nervous systems.

Dr. Leaf's explanations focus more heavily on the way thoughts affect our bodies through the nervous system. Others, such as Henry Wright in his book *A More Excellent Way,*[6] give more details about how our thoughts affect our body through our endocrine systems. Emotions affect the release of hormones, which in turn affects the regulation of the whole body.

Although there are different opinions about the extent to which emotions and thoughts impact our physical health, it's almost undisputed that they have a major effect on our bodies. Fear, anxiety, un-forgiveness, negative thinking patterns, and guilt can all seriously harm a person's physical health. They change the chemistry of the body and weaken the immune system. On the other hand, love and healthy relationships are linked to longer lives, better health, and the ability to overcome great challenges.

---

[4] Lake, John G., and Roberts Liardon. *"Sin In The Flesh."* John G. Lake: The Complete Collection of His Life Teachings. New Kensington, PA: Whitaker House, 2004. 592. Print.
[5] Leaf, Caroline. Who Switched off My Brain?: Controlling Toxic Thoughts and Emotions. Place of Publication Not Identified: Inprov, 2009. Print
[6] Wright, Henry. A More Excellent Way: Pathways of Wholeness Spiritual Roots of Disease. New Kensington, PA: Whitaker House, 2009. Print.

Jesus Has Come In The Flesh

Sin certainly affects the physical body. It isn't just a spiritual thing. Sometimes the affliction comes through the abuse of drugs and alcohol, or a sexually transmitted disease. Sometimes the affliction comes through the effects that fear, guilt, and bitterness have on our bodies through our endocrine and nervous systems.

I don't imply that every sickness is a result of an individual's personal sin. I am saying that sin almost always affects our bodies in some way if it is not dealt with. Most Christians agree that the gospel has provision for deliverance from sin, forgiveness, and freedom from guilt. We receive the free gift of righteousness which results in peace and freedom from mental torment.

Even from a purely natural perspective, without taking miraculous healing into account, it's obvious that anything with the spiritual effect which the gospel has will have a profound redemptive effect on our physical health. Redemption affects the physical body indirectly through the regeneration of the spirit and renewal of the soul. Righteousness, peace, forgiveness, and love affect our physical bodies.

Redemption also affects the physical body directly, through the miraculous working of the Holy Spirit. Scripture teaches physical healing as part of redemption just as plainly as it teaches the forgiveness of sins.

Psalm 103:2-3 Bless the LORD, O my soul, and do not forget all his benefits— who forgives all your iniquity, who heals all your diseases.

Here's a literal translation of Isaiah's prophesy of Jesus. It uses the same Hebrew word when it says Jesus has born our sicknesses, (verse 4) as it does when it says Jesus has born our sin. (verse 12) It also uses the same Hebrew word for *"Jesus carried our pains,"* (verse 4) and *"bore our iniquities."*

2 The Incarnation Shows The Body Is Holy

Isaiah 53:3-6, 10-12 (YLT) He is despised, and left of men, A man of pains, and acquainted with sickness, And as one hiding the face from us, He is despised, and we esteemed him not. Surely our sicknesses he hath borne, And our pains — he hath carried them, And we — we have esteemed him plagued, Smitten of God, and afflicted.

And he is pierced for our transgressions, Bruised for our iniquities, The chastisement of our peace [is] on him, And by his bruise there is healing to us. All of us like sheep have wandered, Each to his own way we have turned, And Jehovah hath caused to meet on him, The punishment of us all...

And Jehovah hath delighted to bruise him, He hath made him sick, If his soul doth make an offering for guilt, He seeth seed — he prolongeth days, And the pleasure of Jehovah in his hand doth prosper.

Of the labour of his soul he seeth — he is satisfied, Through his knowledge give righteousness Doth the righteous one, My servant, to many, And their iniquities he doth bear. Therefore I give a portion to him among the many, And with the mighty he apportioneth spoil, Because that he exposed to death his soul, And with transgressors he was numbered, And he the sin of many hath borne, And for transgressors he intercedeth.

Some translations such as the KJV translate the words in verse 4 as *"griefs"* and *"sorrows"* instead of *"sicknesses"* and *"pains."* However, the first Hebrew word used here, *choliy*,[7] is used 19 times in scripture before Isaiah chapter 53. The KJV denotes it as *"sickness"* or *"disease"* every single time, and the contexts make it clear that it's speaking of physical sickness.

The KJV translates the second of these words, *makob*,[8] as *"pain"* in Job 33:19. It often translates it as *"sorrows"* in other places.

---

[7] Strong, James. *Strong's Hebrew and Greek Dictionaries*, word H2470
[8] Strong's Hebrew and Greek Dictionaries, word H3510

If there's still any doubt, the New Testament refers to the fulfillment of Isaiah's prophesy as healing of physical illness. The only reason to spiritualize the language of Isaiah 53, which talks about physical healing, is bias in translation. The promises seemed too incredible to some translators for them to translate what scripture literally says here.

Matthew 8:14-17 When Jesus entered Peter's house, he saw his mother-in-law lying in bed with a fever; he touched her hand, and the fever left her, and she got up and began to serve him. That evening they brought to him many who were possessed with demons; and he cast out the spirits with a word, and cured all who were sick. This was to fulfill what had been spoken through the prophet Isaiah, "He took our infirmities and bore our diseases."

Even translations which do not translate *choliy* and *makob* as *"sicknesses"* and *"pains"* in Isaiah 53:4 use words referring to physical sickness in the New Testament quotation of Isaiah 53:4. Why? The context makes it so clear in Matthew 8 that there's no escaping the fact it refers to physical sicknesses.

We find another New Testament reference to Isaiah 53 in First Peter. The Greek word used here, translated *"healed,"* is used repeatedly in the gospels, and also in the book of Acts, to describe physical healing miracles.

1 Peter 2:24 He himself bore our sins in his body on the cross, so that, free from sins, we might live for righteousness; by his wounds you have been healed.

Physical healing was so important to Jesus' ministry that Jesus considered it a demonstration of his authority to forgive sins. If people were sick because of their sin, when they were forgiven, it should follow that they would be healed.

Matthew 9:2-8 And just then some people were carrying a paralyzed man lying on a bed. When Jesus saw their faith, he

2 The Incarnation Shows The Body Is Holy

said to the paralytic, "Take heart, son; your sins are forgiven." Then some of the scribes said to themselves, "This man is blaspheming."

But Jesus, perceiving their thoughts, said, "Why do you think evil in your hearts? For which is easier, to say, 'Your sins are forgiven,' or to say, 'Stand up and walk'? But so that you may know that the Son of Man has authority on earth to forgive sins"—he then said to the paralytic—"Stand up, take your bed and go to your home." And he stood up and went to his home. When the crowds saw it, they were filled with awe, and they glorified God, who had given such authority to human beings.

If a person is forgiven of sexual immorality, they should be healed of their AIDS. If a person is forgiven from drunkenness, they should be healed of cirrhosis of the liver. This is the gospel. Yet few people teach it. Jesus also carried the sickness and pain inflicted by other people's sins against us. Salvation is for the spirit, soul, and body.

I have seen marvelous miracles! I've laid my hands on people with histories of alcoholism and nicotine addiction. Several of them have tangibly felt something like a vacuum cleaner cleaning out their livers or lungs. It was a demonstration that their sins were forgiven.

To undermine faith in the gospel message for physical healing is also to undermine faith in the forgiveness offered in the gospel. We may still believe in forgiveness theoretically, but we have a much harder time leading people into real freedom from feelings of guilt and condemnation if we separate physical salvation from forgiveness and salvation of the soul and spirit.

Think of a person who has cancer because of substance abuse, or a person who has a painful STD. Every moment of pain is a reminder of their sin. If Jesus demonstrated the forgiveness of sins by healing every physical effect which would serve as a reminder of that sin, so should we.

Gnostic beliefs proclaim a strict division between body and spirit. However, the human body, soul, and spirit have an interdependent relationship, profoundly affecting one another. Physical sickness can put immense strain on relationships. Couples often divorce after the death of a child. Chronic pain often results in mental torment.

It also works the other way. Mental and emotional torment cause physical pain and physical infirmities. The state of the spirit and soul affect the body. If we reject Christ's redemption for the physical body we undermine the message of his redemption of the soul.

Relegating physical redemption to a future occurrence also delays soul redemption to a future event. I know Christians who don't believe they will ever be free from mental torment or from struggling with sin until they die. They have been taught a theoretical version of salvation; one which lacks a powerful demonstration in this life.

2 Timothy 2:2, 5-6 For people will be lovers of themselves...holding to the outward form of godliness but denying its power. Avoid them! For among them are those who make their way into households and captivate silly women, overwhelmed by their sins and swayed by all kinds of desires

1 Corinthians 4:20 For the kingdom of God depends not on talk but on power.

I've shared only a short summary of the Biblical basis for physical healing as part of salvation; just as relevant as is the forgiveness of sins. We could prove this scripturally from other perspectives as well. F.F. Bosworth gave a more complete scriptural case for the promise of divine healing in his classic book, *Christ The Healer.*[9]

God doesn't wait to forgive our sins. Neither does he wait to heal our bodies. The fact Christians sometimes do sin and some struggle with feelings of guilt and condemnation, does not negate Christ's offer of forgiveness and deliverance from sin. If a young Christian struggles with guilt and

---

[9] Bosworth, F.F. *Christ the Healer*, Grand Rapids: Chosen Books, 2008

condemnation, we don't tell him, *"Well, I guess God didn't choose to forgive you,"* or *"Wait on God's timing, and if he wants, he will forgive you."*

No. We remind the young believer that his feelings may lie, but the gospel is truth. He is forgiven. He is a new creation in Christ. We teach him to stand fast on these truths, and act according to them.

Neither do we tell a believer who is struggling with an addiction that God must not have chosen to deliver him yet. Rather, we apply grace and truth.

We don't say to a struggling Christian, *"Well, if God had chosen to redeem you from sin, you would be free from it."* Yet many believers say to a sick Christian, *"If it had been God's will to heal you, he would have."* Why such inconsistent reasoning? If we stand firmly on the fact that Jesus carried our sins and bore our iniquities, why don't we also stand firmly on the fact that Jesus carried our pains and bore our diseases?

The fact that some Christians have sickness or pain doesn't nullify the fact that Jesus carried our pains and sicknesses on his body. This is no reason to doubt the gospel. Rather, we must apply grace and truth to the situation. God's timing? Scripture is clear about it.

2 Corinthians 6:2 (NIV) For he says, "In the time of my favor I heard you, and in the day of salvation I helped you." I tell you, now is the time of God's favor, now is the day of salvation.

The New Testament uses the same word (sozo) to talk about physical healing and salvation. The Bible talks about physical healing and forgiveness together, using the same language, in the Biblical doctrines of salvation. God doesn't wait to heal people any more than he waits to forgive sin. He has already healed and he has already forgiven. The time of salvation is now. The time for heaven's dominion to be established is now!

Jesus Has Come In The Flesh

Sharing Our Faith With Confidence
For many years, I struggled to share my Christian faith. I sincerely wanted to spread the gospel, but my words felt weak. I loved God and I knew he was real. I knew God had touched me, setting me free from torment and sin. Yet how could I demonstrate this reality to people who didn't believe? How could I show them I had received what other religions could never deliver?

In my early attempts to testify of Jesus I lacked confidence and stumbled over my words. I hardly knew how to begin sharing the gospel, because I didn't know what to say. When I came to understand physical salvation and to heal the sick, sharing the gospel became natural. I became bold, because I had something to show people. Like Jesus did, I could demonstrate the forgiveness of sins through physical healing, calling people to faith in Christ.

Not only that, but I could communicate the love of God to people as never before. Before I learned to minister physical healing, I rarely saw people in tears because of feeling the Lord's love. When I learned to minister physical healing, it became normal to see people weep as their souls were deeply touched by the love of God.

People who were physically healed also experienced *"present salvation"* in their souls. Their hearts were softened. The love of God, communicated through physical healing, can lead people to forgive and to become gentle and patient with others.

As long as my mind was influenced by antichrist teaching— seeing salvation as only a spiritual phenomenon— I was crippled in my ability to share the gospel. This hindered me from demonstrating God's love. An antichrist spirit opposed the anointing in my life by lying to me.

An Antichrist Spirit Teaches Salvation Is For The Spirit And Soul, Not The Body
Just as the Gnostics denied Jesus came in a physical body, an antichrist spirit denies the sanctity of the human body. It

2 The Incarnation Shows The Body Is Holy

applies the promises of salvation for only part of the human being, excluding the body.

An antichrist spirit spiritualizes salvation to make it more theory than tangible, demonstrable reality. Since an antichrist spirit opposes the anointing, it especially works to undermine the aspects of the gospel that can be most readily demonstrated. Such a gospel looks far different than that which Christ proclaimed, because it is in word but not in power.[10]

An antichrist spirit denies the immense value God has for the human body by teaching that Jesus did miracles primarily to prove his divinity. This removes the revelation of the heart and nature of God, demonstrated when Jesus healed the sick.

The greatest revelation of God's value for the human body is that he chose to make his home in our bodies. Of all the places he could choose to dwell, he chose our bodies!

1 Corinthians 6:19-20 Or do you not know that your body is a temple of the Holy Spirit within you, which you have from God, and that you are not your own? For you were bought with a price; therefore glorify God in your body.

We were bought with a price. Jesus shed his blood to redeem us— body, soul, and spirit. Remembering the price Jesus paid reminds us how highly God esteems our physical bodies.

In its most extreme form, the teaching of an antichrist spirit denies a bodily resurrection from the dead. It says the resurrection is only spiritual. Most Christians recognize this as error. However, many do not recognize teaching which removes physical healing from Christ's atonement as equally antichrist in nature.

Physical healing is an essential part of the gospel. Removing healing from the gospel is an antichrist teaching because it denies the sanctity of the physical body. It's also an antichrist teaching for several other reasons, which we'll see in future chapters. Eradicating physical healing from the gospel

---

[10] 1 Corinthians 4:20

message, or saying it has ceased, also denies other implications of Christ's incarnation.

3. Gnosticism, Sex, And The Church
Gnostic Influence In The Church
The view that the spirit is holy but the body is not, was the basis for the Gnostic's denial that Christ came in the flesh. Two extreme views towards sexuality arose from this belief.

The first one said *"My spirit is holy, but my body is evil. Therefore, it doesn't matter what I do with my body. It doesn't affect my spirit."* The result of this belief is gross sexual immorality.

One lie of an antichrist spirit is that it doesn't matter what you do with your body. It claims your body isn't really *"you."* However, Christ demonstrated that the body is holy when he came in a human body.

The second extreme view towards sexuality was *"The body is evil, therefore, sex is evil."* This lie has heavily influenced church history. Many church leaders taught Christians they were sinning if they enjoyed sex with a spouse. Some taught that sex itself was always evil and there was no sex before sin came into the world. In Victorian-era England, women were even taught to complain and bicker with their husbands to avoid the *"evil"* of sex.

This negative view towards sex dates back to the early church. Much of it was due to the influence of the *"Church Fathers."* These included the *"Four Latin Fathers"*— Augustine, Ambrose, Jerome, and Gregory the Great. These were influential Latin-speaking teachers of the early church.

Augustine was possibly the most influential theologian of all time, forming the beliefs of both the Roman Catholic Church and the Protestant Church. Augustine was a member of a Gnostic cult for almost ten years before he became a Christian.

Jesus Has Come In The Flesh

Ambrose was an early church bishop who mentored Augustine. He taught there was no sex before the fall of man, and Adam and Eve had angelic bodies until they sinned, acquiring earthly bodies. His view of the body was the very belief on which the Gnostics based their denial of the incarnation! To his credit, Augustine eventually realized such a belief was incompatible with the doctrines of the bodily resurrection and the incarnation.

Although Augustine eventually rejected the Gnostic belief that the body itself is evil, he continued to teach it was sinful for married couples to be passionate in their sexual relations. Sex was to be a mechanical act, for the purpose of procreation. In fact, Augustine believed that in the Garden of Eden the husband would impregnate his wife by will-power alone, with no loss of her virginity!

Even though Augustine affirmed the body was good, he rejected the physical pleasure of sex as something evil, to be shunned. In this way, Gnosticism continued to influence his teaching. At least he did not reject marriage itself as sinful, but he taught it was inferior to celibacy.

Jerome translated the Bible into Latin. He had an extreme anti-sexual obsession, believing a man could only love his wife if he abstained from all sex with her.

"Matrimony is always a vice. All that can be done is to excuse it and to sanctify it, therefore it was made a religious sacrament"-St. Jerome (347-420)

Jerome harshly opposed a monk named Jovinian, ripping him apart verbally and calling his teaching *"nauseating trash."* What did he think was Jovinian's great error? Jovinian taught that virgins, widows, and married women are of equal merit in Christ, having the same reward in heaven. On the contrary, Jerome believed *"Woman is the root of all evil,"* and that a married woman was on a lower spiritual plane than a virgin.

Gregory the Great was a pope of the early church, called by John Calvin *"the last of the good popes."* He also

3. Gnosticism, Sex, And The Church

had a negative view towards sex, portraying sexual desire as evil. Gregory believed married couples should only have sex for the purpose of procreation. He saw the physical world as a lower realm, to be escaped, and believed physical pleasure would trap a person in this lower realm.

Gregory's views sharply contrast with the truth that Jesus came in the flesh. The body and soul are not at odds with each other. They are closely connected, as both the incarnation and modern science demonstrate. Jesus came to redeem both.

Due to the influence of many early church leaders such as the *"Latin Fathers,"* Christians throughout much of church history have considered it more godly to stay single than to marry. Because influential people taught that enjoying sex was evil, church leaders forbade ministers from marrying. However, scripture calls this a *"doctrine of demons."*

1 Timothy 4:1-5 Now the Spirit expressly says that in later[a] times some will renounce the faith by paying attention to deceitful spirits and teachings of demons, through the hypocrisy of liars whose consciences are seared with a hot iron. They forbid marriage and demand abstinence from foods, which God created to be received with thanksgiving by those who believe and know the truth. For everything created by God is good, and nothing is to be rejected, provided it is received with thanksgiving; for it is sanctified by God's word and by prayer.

The body is holy, and sex is holy. The lie that it's evil has caused tremendous damage throughout history. The fruit of this lie is also sexual immorality and perversion. Prostitution often abounds in a society where sex is considered evil. Perversion and sexual addiction also take root in such a society.

If sex with your spouse is a *"necessary evil,"* what is the difference between that and having sex with someone who isn't your spouse? People who learn that all sex is evil become frustrated and confused. Many give up and abandon themselves to any and every desire. Vilification of that which is holy produces immorality, not holiness.

Gnostic influence on the beliefs of the church regarding sexuality has historically set the stage for *"sexual revolution."* Many people reacted to the Gnostic teaching that sex is evil by embracing immorality. They sought freedom but instead found pain and more bondage.

If the antichrist spirit can't convince you it doesn't matter what you do with your body, it will try to convince you that all sex is evil. Both lies are based on the lie that the body is vile.

In the last several decades, the church has made great progress with breaking free from this negative view towards the body. The influence of a Gnostic, antichrist view of the body was so strong only a couple decades ago, Brazilian Christians often considered soccer a sinful activity! Many people thought a person could not be a Christian and be involved in sports. Rampant sexual immorality, both inside and outside the church, is a reflection on the influence of those antichrist teachings.

Glorify God With Your Body — Because Jesus Has Come In Your Flesh

When the Bible tells us to be sexually pure, the reason is because our bodies are holy. The fact that Jesus has come in the flesh is a basis for sexual purity.

1 Corinthians 6:15-20 Do you not know that your bodies are members of Christ? Should I therefore take the members of Christ and make them members of a prostitute? Never!

Do you not know that whoever is united to a prostitute becomes one body with her? For it is said, "The two shall be one flesh." But anyone united to the Lord becomes one spirit with him.

Shun fornication! Every sin that a person commits is outside the body; but the fornicator sins against the body itself. Or do you not know that your body is a temple of the Holy

3. Gnosticism, Sex, And The Church

Spirit within you, which you have from God, and that you are not your own? For you were bought with a price; therefore glorify God in your body.

Why do we shun sexual immorality? Because our bodies are members of Christ! Christ not only came in the flesh, but he has come in our flesh! Our bodies are temples of the Holy Spirit. This is basis for sexual morality. Sexual morality is really what's natural, because we're wired for it. It's the natural outcome of understanding the sacredness and value of the human body.

An antichrist spirit degrades the body and desensitizes people to its worth. It not only denies Jesus came in the flesh. It also denies Jesus has come in our flesh. It denies that the spirit of Christ lives in the body of the one who has faith in Christ.

In the last chapter I mentioned how denying the physical aspect of salvation tends to create a version of the gospel that's theory but has little power. Notice the next thing that scripture says about those who deny the gospel's power.

2 Timothy 2:2, 5-6 For people will be lovers of themselves...holding to the outward form of godliness but denying its power. Avoid them! For among them are those who make their way into households and captivate silly women, overwhelmed by their sins and swayed by all kinds of desires

Paul said there were seducers among those who denied the power of the gospel. An antichrist spirit promotes sexual immorality by presenting a form of godliness that is only *"spiritual"* but has no power.

4. An Antichrist Spirit Promotes Sexual Immorality And Violence

Counterfeits

We're going to cover some heavy material in this section. I want to preface it with a reminder that the devil is a counterfeiter —and the things he most distorts are the most sacred and wonderful things in the form God created them.

Our sexuality is wonderful. It reflects God's nature, creates families, and brings life. The oneness God created a man and a woman to share points to the union between Christ and the church. The marriage bed is holy[11]—and God wants you to have fun in bed with your spouse! Remember: Our sexuality as God created it to function brings just as much life as the devil's perversion of sexuality brings death.

As we examine how extensive the damage from desensitization and Satan's perversion of sexuality is, remember this is how things work under the law of sin and death—which Jesus sets us free from.[12] God is able to save you completely,[13] and his redemption goes far deeper than any work of the devil.

I've heard countless testimonies of people who were caught in the depths of sin and despair, and Jesus totally redeemed their lives and undid the works of the devil. As Betsie Ten Boom said, *"No pit is so deep that he is not deeper*

---

[11] Hebrews 13:4
[12] Romans 8:2
[13] Hebrews 7:25

still."[14] God forgives and throws our sins into the depths of the sea, never to be remembered again.[15] He restores hearts, relationships, and everything Satan stole, so that you end up having twice as much as you did before you ever lost anything.[16] He's a wonderful Savior!

If you can relate to the painful effects of desensitization related in this chapter, remember that all of these are the things which Jesus came in the flesh to undo. This is an account of what Jesus redeems you from, and it's an account of the areas where you will bring redemption to people around you as you understand the truth of the incarnation. These are the reasons we must declare and demonstrate that Jesus has come in the flesh!

The Body-Soul-Spirit Connection And Sexuality

We've noted that an antichrist spirit separates physical healing from salvation, just as the Gnostics taught a dichotomy between the body and the rest of the being. This dichotomy relates to sexuality as well. It's a lie that what you do with your body is just physical.

Ephesians 4:17 tells us to *"no longer live as the gentiles do, in the futility of their thinking."* The next verse goes on to describe the result of being blinded and separated from God's life — desensitization leading to immorality.

Ephesians 4:18-19 (NIV) They are darkened in their understanding and separated from the life of God because of the ignorance that is in them due to the hardening of their hearts. Having lost all sensitivity they have given themselves over to sensuality so as to indulge in every form of impurity...

We discussed how emotions, thought patterns, and relationships affect our physical bodies. This is one reason

---

[14] Boom, Corrie Ten; Elizabeth Sherrill; John Sherrill. *The Hiding Place* (p. 227). Baker Publishing Group. Kindle Edition.
[15] Micah 7:19
[16] Job 42:10

4. An Antichrist Spirit Promotes Sexual Immorality And Violence

salvation which is only *"spiritual"* is salvation in theory, not reality. On the other hand, what we do with our physical bodies, especially with our sexuality, also affects our brains, emotions, and ability to have healthy relationships. It affects our ability to love and have natural affection.

Sex releases various hormones in the body. These include oxytocin and vasopressin, which play a role in bonding and empathy. They not only create a bond between a husband and wife, but between parents and their children. They also function in other relationships.

Some animals have many mates, and others mate for life. This is due to physical differences in their brains and biology. Some animals are wired to have multiple mates, and others are wired for monogamy. Humans are wired to be faithful to one partner.

Scientists have performed experiments with animals like prairie voles that are wired for monogamous relationships. By blocking the effect of vasopressin in the males, or of oxytocin in the females, scientists were able to prevent the normal pair-bonding from occurring with mates.[17]

The body also releases other hormones during sex, such as dopamine. Our whole bodies are regulated by hormones. Hormones involved in sex also have other functions in the body.

Our sexual choices affect our emotional and physical well-being through physical processes. There are good and bad choices for how we use our sexuality. Frequent sex in a marriage relationship is, in general, great for both physical health and emotional well-being. Bad choices, such as pornography, damage physical health and emotional well-being. For example, here's a quote from a 2012 letter[18] written by Rui Miguel Costa.

---

[17] http://www.americanscientist.org/issues/pub/high-on-fidelity
[18] http://www.reuniting.info/download/pdf/Costa.Masturbation.PDF

"It is difficult to reconcile the view that masturbation improves mood with the findings in both sexes that greater masturbation frequency is associated with more depressive symptoms,[19] less happiness,[20] and several other indicators of poorer physical and mental health, which include anxious attachment,[21] immature psychological defense mechanisms, greater blood pressure reactivity to stress, and dissatisfaction with one's mental health and life in general.[22].

It is equally difficult to see how masturbation develops sexual interests, when greater masturbation frequency is so often associated with impaired sexual function in men[23] and women.[24] Greater masturbation frequency is also associated with more dissatisfaction with relationships and less love for partners.[25] In contrast, PVI (penile-vaginal intercourse) is very consistently related to better health,[26] better sexual function,[27] and better intimate relationship quality[28]... The only sexual behavior consistently related to better psychological and physical health is PVI."

A wealth of research shows the damage pornography use causes. Real sex involves the whole person. Real sex involves pheromones, touching, and an emotional connection. Just as an antichrist spirit does, sexual addiction separates the body from the rest of the being. It makes the body out to be only material,

---

[19] Cyranowski et al., 2004; Frohlich & Meston, 2002; Husted & Edwards, 1976
[20] Das, 2007
[21] Costa & Brody, 2011
[22] For a review, see Brody, 2010
[23] Brody & Costa, 2009; Das, Parish, & Laumann, 2009; Gerressu, Mercer, Graham, Wellings, & Johnson, 2008; Lau, Wang, Cheng, & Yang, 2005; Nutter & Condron, 1985
[24] Brody & Costa, 2009; Das et al., 2009; Gerressu et al., 2008; Lau, Cheng, Wang, & Yang, 2006; Shaeer, Shaeer, & Shaeer, 2012; Weiss & Brody, 2009
[25] Brody, 2010; Brody & Costa, 2009
[26] Brody, 2010; Brody & Costa, 2009; Brody & Weiss, 2011; Costa & Brody, 2011, 2012
[27] (Brody & Costa, 2009; Brody & Weiss, 2011; Nutter & Condron, 1983, 1985; Weiss & Brody, 2009
[28] Brody, 2010; Brody & Costa, 2009; Brody & Weiss, 2011

4. An Antichrist Spirit Promotes Sexual Immorality And Violence

as opposed to being sacred and closely linked to the soul and spirit of the person.

Sexual immorality, especially pornography, breaks down the ability to create healthy bonds with people. It erodes natural affection and destroys relationships. It de-sensitizes people and decreases empathy, reducing sex to much less than the wonderful gift God created it to be. Much research confirms this.

After consumption of pornography, subjects reported less satisfaction with their intimate partners—specifically, with these partners' affection, physical appearance, sexual curiosity, and sexual performance proper. In addition, subjects assigned increased importance to sex without emotional involvement. These effects were uniform across gender and populations.[29]

Research has shown that the brain scans of people addicted to pornography look like the brain scans of people addicted to drugs. Although there are some who continue to claim pornography is harmless, the evidence is mounting against them. Instead of giving extensive citations of studies and quotations, I list a few websites at the end of this chapter for readers who want to learn more.

Some compare pornography today with tobacco or cocaine use in the past. There was a time when both cocaine and tobacco were considered harmless, even beneficial. Even as the evidence mounted against them, people continued to insist these toxins were harmless. In the same way, we now have strong evidence of the harm caused by pornography. However, many people continue to insist, against all reason, that porn is harmless.

---

[29] Zillmann, D. and Bryant, J. (1988), Pornography's Impact on Sexual Satisfaction. Journal of Applied Social Psychology, 18: 438–453. doi: 10.1111/j.1559-1816.1988.tb00027.x

Gary Wilson, author of the book *"Your Brain on Porn,"* said the following in his TED talk *"The Great Porn Experiment."*[30]

Arousal addiction symptoms are easily mistaken for such things as ADHD, social anxiety, depression, concentration problems, performance anxiety, OCD and a host of others.

Now, healthcare providers often assume that these conditions are primary, perhaps the cause of addiction, but never really the result of an addiction. As a consequence they often medicate these guys without really inquiring about if they have an Internet addiction.

Guys never realize that they could overcome these symptoms simply by changing their behavior.

Even without the research, many people know the fruits of lust and sexual immorality by painful experience. Low self-esteem, self-hatred, and self-harm often go together with promiscuity.

"Promiscuity is the main thing," Dr. (Steve) Perry says in Oprah's Lifeclass,"on the topic of daddyless daughters. "It's rarely seen as self-mutilation, but that's exactly what it is."

Iyanla Vanzant, a prominent voice in the discussion on both daddyless daughters and fatherless sons, agrees. "Absolutely. It's violence against the self," she says.

Dr. Perry continues, "Often when we look at young girls who are dealing with pain, we think of self-mutilation as the cutting. That, too, but promiscuity is the self-mutilation of allowing someone to physically enter you."

"Wow, that's a big one," Oprah says. "Self-mutilation comes in the form of promiscuity and its violence against the self. I never thought of it that way before."[31]

Of course *"allowing someone to physically enter you"* in the context of trust and commitment (marriage) isn't self-harm.

---

[30] http://yourbrainonporn.com/garys-tedx-talk-great-porn-experiment
[31] Watson, Beth. *Is Promiscuity A Form Of Self-Mutilation?* Online. http://www.counseling4less.com/blog/promiscuity-a-form-of self-mutilation

4. An Antichrist Spirit Promotes Sexual Immorality And Violence

It's a wonderful thing! But when sex is separated from commitment and intimacy, it becomes self-harm. Paul wrote to the Corinthians that the one who sins sexually sins against his own body! So many people have found themselves feeling numb and wounded after sexual sin! Culture and society lied to them by depicting a twisted view of sexuality.

Just as physically abusing one's self is possible, by activities such as cutting or head-banging, it's possible to sexually abuse one's self. That's what sexual immorality is—self-abuse. An antichrist spirit hates the body, because God chose the human body to be his temple. Therefore, antichrist promotes anything that harms the body. Lust often goes hand-in-hand with violence. They come from the same spirit.

In fact, in the study of popular porn videos, in nine scenes out of 10, a women was being hit, beaten, yelled at, or otherwise harmed, and the result was almost always the same—the victim either seemed not to mind or looked happy about it.[32]

Here's a quote from an ex porn star. Many people who are hurting because of the misuse of sex turn to drugs to numb the pain. Thus they hurt themselves even more. In contrast to this, everything the incarnation implies is diametrically opposed to the spirit of lust.

"You're viewed as an object and not as a human with a spirit," wrote Jersey Jaxin, a former porn star that left the industry in 2007. "People do drugs because they can't deal with the way they are being treated. Seventy five percent [of porn performers] and rising are using drugs. Have to numb themselves.

There are specific doctors in this industry that if you go in for a common cold they'll give you Vicodin, Viagra,

---

[32] Bridges, A. J., Wosnitzer, R., Scharrer, E., Chyng, S., and Liberman, R. (2010). Aggression and Sexual Behavior in Best Selling Pornography Videos: A Content Analysis Update. Violence Against Women 16, 10: 1065–1085.

anything you want because all they care about is the money. You are a number. You're bruised. You have black eyes. You're ripped. You're torn. You have your insides coming out." [33]

Here are a few more statistics, thanks to the site wf-lawyers.com.[34] Notice the relationship between early sexual choices and the ability to have a stable marriage in the future.

- *60 percent of cohabiting couples will eventually marry. However, living together prior to marriage can increase the chance of getting divorced by as much as 40 percent.*

- *If you are a female serial cohabiter – a woman who has lived with more than one partner before your first marriage – then you're 40 percent more likely to get divorced than women who have never done so.*

- *Women who lost their virginity as a teenager are more than twice as likely to get divorce in the first 5 years of marriage than women who waited until age 18 or older.*

- *A 2011 study at the University of Iowa found that for both men and women, the loss of virginity before age 18 was correlated with a greater number of occurrences of divorce within the first 10 years of marriage.*

- *When compared to women who began sexual activity in their early 20s, girls who initiated sexual activity at ages 13 or 14 were less than half as likely to be in stable marriages in their 30s. – (in this study a stable marriage was defined as a marriage of over five years).*

- *Women with 6 or more pre-marital sexual partners are almost 3 times less likely to be in a stable marriage.*

---

[33] Jersey Jaxin *Former Porn Star Jersey Jaxin Story* Online.
https://www.shelleylubben.com/former-porn-star-jersey-jaxin-story
[34] Online. http://www.wf-lawyers.com/divorce-statistics-and-facts/

4. An Antichrist Spirit Promotes Sexual Immorality And Violence

• *Pornography addiction was cited as a factor in 56 percent of divorces according to a recent study.*

• *Having a baby before marriage can increase risk of divorce by 24 percent.*

As you continue to read these statistics from wf-lawyers.com, consider some of the other consequences of divorce. Consider the pain of living in poverty, and the further stress it puts on the remaining relationships.
Consider how seriously broken relationships harm physical health. The effects of this reach even further. If a person dies early, friends and other family members suffer. Think about the social costs involved, and the burden on taxpayers.

• *Families with children that were not poor before the divorce see their income drop as much as 50 percent.*

• *Almost 50 percent of the parents with children that are going through a divorce move into poverty after the divorce.*

• *A new study entitled "Divorce and Death" shows that broken marriages can kill at the same rate as smoking cigarettes. Indications that the risk of dying is a full 23 percent higher among divorcées than married people.*

• *One researcher determined that a single divorce costs state and federal governments about $30,000, based on such things as the higher use of food stamps and public housing as well as increased bankruptcies and juvenile delinquency.*

• *The nation's 1.4 million divorces in 2002 are estimated to have cost the taxpayers more than $30 billion.*

Jesus Has Come In The Flesh

The purpose of calling these facts to attention is not to point the finger at anyone to remind them of their past. We have all made choices that hurt ourselves, and we have all experienced brokenness. Rather, understanding how far-reaching the consequences of sexual immorality are, helps us to get a vision of how far redemption reaches when God delivers people from desensitization and sexual brokenness.

In spite of all the glorification of sexual immorality, a growing *"No Fap"* movement has sprung up in recent years. *"Fap"* is a term for solo-sex. No-Fappers make a commitment to abstain from pornography and masturbation. This is called *"rebooting."*[35] Many no-Fappers are atheists. Others have religious beliefs. The main motivation for abstaining from solo-sex is that people feel bad with it! They realize it is hurting them.

People who *"reboot"* often report increased confidence, a surge in physical energy, increased creativity, decrease in social anxiety and anxiety in general, increased empathy, freedom from feelings of shame, improvement in mood, and more. Many have recovered from erectile dysfunction. People are quitting solo-sex because they feel so much better without it!

It's tragic that sexual choices which lead to such pain have been glorified and encouraged. It's sad that many have been duped to embrace a view of sex that ignores the connection between body, soul, and spirit. It should be clear that just as there are healthy and unhealthy choices we make with food, there are healthy and unhealthy sexual choices, affecting every aspect of our lives.

So what's my point in delving into the harm caused by sexual immorality? Remember, the Gnostics denied Jesus came in the flesh because they argued against the sanctity of the body. I've expounded on some mechanisms by which an antichrist spirit destroys. It's evident that we can extensively impact every area of society by demonstrating that Jesus has come in the flesh. Let's look at a few more ways sexual

---

[35] https://www.nofap.com/rebooting/

4. An Antichrist Spirit Promotes Sexual Immorality And Violence

immorality contributes to the problems of today's society. I believe the most significant of these is fatherlessness.

Fatherlessness

Sexual immorality causes more fatherlessness than any other factor. Most fatherlessness is due to birth out of wedlock, or divorce. Of course, birth out of wedlock results from extramarital or premarital sex, biblically termed adultery, or fornication.

What about divorce? We've already reviewed statistics demonstrating that premarital sex, cohabitation, having a baby before marriage, and the number of sexual partners before marriage, all drastically increase the probability of divorce. We've discussed one of the mechanisms by which this occurs, which is a breakdown in the ability to bond in a healthy way and experience empathy and natural affection.

We saw that pornography addiction is cited as a factor in 56 percent of divorces. Of course, many divorces are also caused by sexual infidelity. But even in those divorces where neither spouse cheated on each other, how much did lust or sexual addiction contribute to the divorce?

We know porn use decreases satisfaction with spouses, decreases perception of a spouse's attractiveness, decreases trust, and decreases empathy and the ability to love. Is loss of trust and empathy a factor in relational frustration and arguments? Is decreased perception of a spouse's attractiveness a factor in boredom with the relationship? Yes.

One 2009 study could not find a control group of men in their 20's who didn't use porn.[36] I think it's reasonable to assume lust and sexual sin are major contributors to most divorces, even the ones not directly caused by an affair.

Since the two main causes of fatherlessness are birth out of wedlock and divorce, it's evident that most fatherlessness is a result of sexual sin. Statistics of

---

[36] University of Montreal. (2009, December 1). Are the effects of pornography negligible?. *ScienceDaily*. Retrieved July 6, 2016 from www.sciencedaily.com/releases/2009/12/091201111202.htm

Jesus Has Come In The Flesh

fatherlessness make it clear how extensive the effects of sexual immorality are. We'll start with a collection of facts from *Getting Men Involved*— the newsletter of the Bay Area Male Involvement Network.[37]

- *63% of youth suicides are from fatherless homes (Source: U.S. D.H.H.S., Bureau of the Census*

- *90% of all homeless and runaway children are from fatherless homes*

- *85% of all children that exhibit behavioral disorders come from fatherless homes (Source: Center for Disease Control)*

- *80% of rapists motivated with displaced anger come from fatherless homes (Source: Criminal Justice & Behavior, Vol 14, p. 403-26, 1978.)*

- *71% of all high school dropouts come from fatherless homes (Source: National Principals Association Report on the State of High Schools.)*

- *75% of all adolescent patients in chemical abuse centers come from fatherless homes (Source: Rainbows for all God's Children.)*

- *70% of juveniles in state-operated institutions come from fatherless homes (Source: U.S. Dept. of Justice, Special Report, Sept 1988)*

- *85% of all youths sitting in prisons grew up in a fatherless home (Source: Fulton Co. Georgia jail populations, Texas Dept. of Corrections 1992)*

---

[37] *Getting Men Involved,* Spring 1997. Online. Retrieved July 19, 2016 from http://www.fathermag.com/news/2778-stats.shtml

4. An Antichrist Spirit Promotes Sexual Immorality And Violence

(Because only a portion of each age group grew up in a fatherless home,) these statistics translate to mean that children from fatherless homes are:

5 times more likely to commit suicide
32 times more likely to run away
20 times more likely to have behavioral disorders
14 times more likely to commit rape
9 times more likely to drop out of high school
10 times more likely to abuse chemical substances
9 times more likely to end up in a state-operated institution
20 times more likely to end up in prison."

These statistics show a strong correlation of fatherlessness with suicide, homelessness, behavioral disorders, sexual violence, dropping out of high school, substance abuse, and crime. Here are some more statistics to consider, compiled by www.fathers.com.[38]

• *Children in father-absent homes are almost four times more likely to be poor. In 2011, 12 percent of children in married-couple families were living in poverty, compared to 44 percent of children in mother-only families.*[39]

• *Children in grades 7-12 who have lived with at least one biological parent, youth that experienced divorce, separation, or nonunion birth reported lower grade point averages than those who have always lived with both biological parents.*

---

[38] Online. http://www.fathers.com/statistics-and-research/the-consequences-of-fatherlessness
[39] U.S. Census Bureau, Children's Living Arrangements and Characteristics: March 2011, Table C8. Washington D.C.: 2011.

- *Children living with their married biological father tested at a significantly higher level than those living with a non-biological father.*[40]

- *Children age 10 to 17 living with two biological or adoptive parents were significantly less likely to experience sexual assault, child maltreatment, other types of major violence, and non-victimization type of adversity, and were less likely to witness violence in their families compared to peers living in single-parent families and stepfamilies.*[41]

- *A study using a sample of 1409 rural southern adolescents (851 females and 558 males) aged 11 – 18 years, investigated the correlation between father absence and self-reported sexual activity. The results revealed that adolescents in father-absence homes were more likely to report being sexually active compared to adolescents living with their fathers.*[42]

- *Being raised by a single mother raises the risk of teen pregnancy, marrying with less than a high school degree, and forming a marriage where both partners have less than a high school degree.*[43]

Here are two additional statistics. They show the strong correlation between fatherlessness and crime and promiscuity.

---

[40] Tillman, K. H. (2007). Family structure pathways and academic disadvantage among adolescents in stepfamilies. Journal of Marriage and Family.

[41] Source: Heather A. Turner, *"The Effect of Lifetime Victimization on the Mental Health of Children and Adolescents,"* Social Science & Medicine, Vol. 62, No. 1, (January 2006), pp. 13-27.

[42] Source: Hendricks, C.S., Cesario, S.K., Murdaugh, C., Gibbons, M.E., Servonsky, E.J., Bobadilla, R.V., Hendricks, D.L., Spencer-Morgan, B., & Tavakoli, A. (2005).

[43] Source: Teachman, Jay D. *"The Childhood Living Arrangements of Children and the Characteristics of Their Marriages."* Journal of Family Issues 25 (January 2004): 86-111.

4. An Antichrist Spirit Promotes Sexual Immorality And Violence

- *A study of 263 13- to 18-year-old adolescent women seeking psychological services found that the adolescents from father-absent homes were 3.5 times more likely to experience pregnancy than were adolescents from father-present homes. Moreover, the rate of pregnancy among adolescents from father absent homes was 17.4% compared to a four (4) percent rate in the general adolescent population.*[44]

- *Researchers using secondary data from the Interuniversity Consortium for Political and Social Research examined gun carrying and drug trafficking in young men, linking father absence to the likelihood of engaging in these behaviors. Results from a sample of 835 juvenile male inmates found that father absence was the only disadvantage on the individual level with significant effects on gun carrying, drug trafficking, and co-occurring behavior. Individuals from father absent homes were found to be 279% more likely to carry guns and deal drugs than peers living with their fathers.*[45]

All these statistics highlight the relationship between fatherlessness and poverty, poor academic performance, sexual assault, domestic violence, and promiscuity. These problems are a vicious cycle. Sexual immorality leads to breakdown in natural affection and relationships, which leads to more sexual immorality and self-destructive behavior as kids are raised without fathers. Jesus came in the flesh to break this cycle.

Physical health problems are also attributed to fatherlessness. In the previous chapter, we discussed how an antichrist spirit denies the redemption of the body as part of

---

[44] Lang, D. L., Rieckmann, T., DiClemente, R. J., Crosby, R. A., Brown, L. K., & Donenberg, G. R. (2013). *Multi-level factors associated with pregnancy among urban adolescent women seeking psychological services.* Journal of Urban Health, 90, 212-223.

[45] Allen, A. N., & Lo, C. C. (2012). *Drugs, guns, and disadvantaged youths: Co-occurring behavior and the code of the street.* Crime & Delinquency, 58(6), 932-953.

Christ's atonement. Because antichrist hates the body, it promotes sickness and disease. Satan comes to steal, to kill, and to destroy.[46]

- *Fatherless children experience more accidents and a higher rate of chronic asthma, headaches, and speech defects.*[47]

- *A study of 1,397,801 infants in Florida evaluated how a lack of father involvement impacts infant mortality. A lack of father involvement was linked to earlier births as well as lower birth weights. Researchers also found that father absence increases the risk of infant mortality, and that the mortality rate for infants within the first 28 days of life is four times higher for those with absent fathers than those with involved fathers. Paternal absence is also found to increase black/white infant mortality almost four-fold.*[48]

STDs/STIs

When discussing the impact of our sexual choices, we can't forget to mention the damage caused by STDs, (Sexually Transmitted Diseases) or, as some prefer to call them, STIs. (Sexually Transmitted Infections) Sexually transmitted diseases are an epidemic. The distress caused by them is tremendous. Cancer, pain, infertility, shame, vulnerability to other diseases, and many deaths are among the results of STDs.

One of the most destructive STDs is HIV. Some African countries have an HIV rate of over 20%. In places with

---

[46] John 10:10
[47] Harknett, Kristin. *Children's Elevated Risk of Asthma in Unmarried Families: Underlying Structural and Behavioral Mechanisms.* Working Paper #2005-01-FF. Princeton, NJ: Center for Research on Child Well-being, 2005: 19-27
[48] Alio, A. P., Mbah, A. K., Kornosky, J. L., Wathington, D., Marty, P. J., & Salihu, H. M. (2011). *Assessing the impact of paternal involvement on Racial/Ethnic disparities in infant mortality rates.* Journal of Community Health, 36(1), 63-68.

4. An Antichrist Spirit Promotes Sexual Immorality And Violence

very high rates of HIV, the disease affects whole communities and exacerbates problems such as poverty.

STDs are a serious problem not only in Africa, but in most of the world. Here are some statistics compiled by the ASHA. (American Sexual Health Association)[49]

- *More than half of all people will have an STD/STI at some point in their lifetime.*[50]

- *The total estimated direct cost of STIs annually in the U.S. is $15.6 billion (2010 US dollars).*[51]

- *Each year, one in four teens contracts an STD/STI.*[52]

- *One in two sexually active persons will contract an STD/STI by age 25.*[53]

- *About half of all new STDs/STIs in 2000 occurred among youth ages 15 to 24.7 The total estimated costs of these nine million new cases of these STDs/STIs was $6.5 billion, with HIV and human papillomavirus (HPV) accounting for 90% of the total burden.*[54]

- *Of the STDs/STIs that are diagnosed, only some (gonorrhea, syphilis, chlamydia, hepatitis A and B) are*

---

[49] Online. http://www.ashasexualhealth.org/stdsstis/statistics/
[50] Koutsky L. (1997). *Epidemiology of genital human papillomavirus infection.* American Journal of Medicine, 102(5A), 3-8.
[51] Owusu-Edusei K, et al. The estimated direct medical cost of selected sexually transmitted infections in the United States, 2008. Sex Transm Dis 2013; 40(3): pp. 197-201
[52] Alan Guttmacher Institute. (1994). *Sex and America's Teenagers.* New York: Alan Guttmacher Institute.
[53] Cates JR, Herndon NL, Schulz S L, Darroch JE. (2004). *Our voices, our lives, our futures: Youth and sexually transmitted diseases.* Chapel Hill, NC: University of North Carolina at Chapel Hill School of Journalism and Mass Communication.
[54] Chesson HW, Blandford JM, Gift TL, Tao G, Irwin KL. (2004). *The estimated direct medical cost of sexually transmitted diseases among American youth,* 2000. Perspectives on Sexual and Reproductive Health, 36, 11-19.

required to be reported to state health departments and the CDC.

- *One out of 20 people in the United States will get infected with hepatitis B (HBV) some time during their lives.*[55] *Hepatitis B is 100 times more infectious than HIV.*[56]

- *Approximately half of HBV infections are transmitted sexually.*[57] *HBV is linked to chronic liver disease, including cirrhosis and liver cancer.*

Again, think of how far the damage caused by STD's reaches. What else could be done with the billions of dollars spent treating them? How much untold harm have relationships suffered because of the stress and suffering caused by these physical diseases?

This series of books is all about making the earth like heaven. If we are going to undo the works of the devil, we must understand how harm has been done as to know how it can be undone. What's the best way to prevent STDs, besides not having any sex at all? According to the ASHA:

Mutual monogamy (only having sex with your partner) is another way to limit exposure to STIs. If neither partner has ever had sexual contact of any kind with another person, there is no risk of STIs.[58]

---

[55] Centers for Disease Control and Prevention. *Hepatitis B Frequently Asked Questions.* Updated April 1, 2005. Retrieved April 22, 2005 from http://www.cdc.gov/ncidod/diseases/hepatitis/b/faqb.htm
[56] Centers for Disease Control and Prevention. *Hepatitis B Prevention for Men Who Have Sex With Men. Online Fact Sheet.* Updated April 1, 2005. Retrieved April 22, 2005 from
http://www.cdc.gov/ncidod/diseases/hepatitis/msm/hbv_msm_fact.htm
[57] Centers for Disease Control and Prevention. *Tracking the hidden epidemics, 2000: Trends in the United States.* Retrieved April 22, 2005 from http://www.cdc.gov/nchstp/od/news/RevBrochure1pdfHepatitisB.htm.
[58] Online. http://www.ashasexualhealth.org/stdsstis/prevention-tips/

4. An Antichrist Spirit Promotes Sexual Immorality And Violence

How are people going to commit to mutual monogamy? As we've seen, we are biologically wired for it. If promiscuity and lust stem from desensitization and the lies of an antichrist spirit about the body, people must be re-sensitized and taught that the body is holy.

Violence And Substance Abuse

We discussed the two main causes of fatherlessness — birth out of wedlock, and divorce. We talked about the role of sexual immorality in divorce, expounding on how far the consequences of sexual immorality extend. Violence and substance abuse are two more causes of divorce and fatherlessness. They are both closely related to sexual immorality.

A spirit of violence involves the same separation between the body and the rest of the human being as does a spirit of sexual immorality. The same lie is behind immorality, violence, and substance abuse. It's the lie of a spirit that denies the incarnation by denying the sanctity of the human body. The same lie separates the physical body from the rest of the person in relation to the atonement and salvation. On the contrary, the incarnation demonstrates the body is holy.

Richard Wurmbrand wrote about how communist torturers responded when asked if they had any compassion. Their response is a good example of an antichrist spirit's teaching about the body, and what that teaching implies:

When Wurmbrand asked if they felt any pity, the torturers replied with quotations from Lenin, like *"You cannot make omelets without breaking the shells of eggs"* and *"You cannot cut wood without making chips fly."*

Wurmbrand responded by saying that wood feels nothing when we cut it, but human beings feel pain. Yet his reply was in vain.

After recounting this story, Wurmbrand explained that communists are materialists. Only matter exists to them. They fall to unimaginable depths of cruelty, because they've been desensitized to think of a man as if he's no different than wood or an eggshell.[59]

The same antichrist, materialistic attitude behind the Communist philosophy made sex a taboo subject in Communist Russia. It was a set-up for sexual immorality. Promiscuity and immorality increased. Since the fall of Communism, Russia has become one of the leading nations of the world in divorce and sexual infidelity. In fact, many Russians accept adultery as normal. Russia now has a large number of orphans and a whole host of social problems which come with fatherlessness.

Like sexual immorality, both violent behavior and substance abuse involve a loss in empathy and result in physical changes in the brain and body chemistry. As we've seen, sexual immorality can lead to both violence and substance abuse.

One the other hand, violence and substance abuse contribute to divorce, which increases the probability of the children becoming promiscuous. Therefore, violence and substance abuse are also factors in setting the stage for sexual immorality. All of these problems are part of a vicious cycle. They exacerbate each other.

We can trace every major problem in our societies to the influence of an antichrist spirit. It denies the incarnation and denies the sanctity of the body. Every spirit that is not of God denies Jesus has come in the flesh. Every spirit that is of God acknowledges Jesus has come in the flesh.

We discussed how the teaching of the Gnostics influenced the church fathers' view of sexuality. Religious violence, the inquisition, and the torture of dissidents can also be traced back to the influence of the Gnostics.

The church historian Neander said Augustine's teaching *"contains the germ of the whole system of spiritual despotism, intolerance, and persecution, even to the court of the Inquisition."* Augustine suggested bringing men to God by

---

[59] Wurmbrand, Richard. Tortured for Christ (Kindle Locations 640-645). Living Sacrifice Book Company. Kindle Edition.

4. An Antichrist Spirit Promotes Sexual Immorality And Violence

fear of pain if *"instruction"* did not work, and argued that the state should have the power to punish religious error.

Augustine's teachings not only engendered violence in the Catholic Church, but in the Protestant Church as well. His teaching heavily influenced Martin Luther and John Calvin, who also used violence to enforce religious conformity. The influence of Martin Luther, in turn, helped to set the stage for the holocaust.

Ambrose, Augustine's mentor, showed anti-Semitic sentiment and a disposition to use violence to enforce religious conformity. He once stated it was not a crime to burn down a synagogue. According to James Carroll, Ambrose *"wanted to kill Jews (since, after all, Christian heretics were being killed for denying details of orthodoxy, while Jews rejected the whole of it)."*[60]

I want to note, for the sake of accuracy, that men like Augustine and Martin Luther did have changing views. It seems Augustine got better with time, and Martin Luther got worse. Augustine has probably influenced church history more than any other theologian, and some of his teaching caused a lot of harm. However, Augustine actually had less extreme views about sexuality and a more positive attitude overall towards Jews than some of the other church fathers.

Although he opposed Gnosticism, Augustine never fully broke away from the Gnostic way of thinking or from Greek philosophy. Yet over time he made some steps in the right direction, especially when he rejected the notion that the body itself was evil. To his credit, he realized this idea was incompatible with the incarnation and the resurrection of the body.

Loss Of Natural Affection

In Romans chapter 1, Paul said God's invisible qualities are revealed in his creation, that is, the natural world. The natural,

---

[60] Carroll, James. Page 104. *Jerusalem, Jerusalem: how the ancient city ignited our modern world.* Houghton Mifflin Harcourt. 2011. Print.

physical realm reveals God. The human body especially reveals God. Jesus revealed God the Father by coming in a physical, human body.

Romans 1:19-20 For what can be known about God is plain to them, because God has shown it to them. Ever since the creation of the world his eternal power and divine nature, invisible though they are, have been understood and seen through the things he has made. So they are without excuse.

The chapter continues to describe how men rejected the knowledge of God and exchanged the truth of God for a lie, so they became depraved. Note this: if God reveals himself to men through his physical creation, rejecting the physical realm as evil is rejecting the knowledge of God. This is exactly what the Gnostics did. They taught the physical realm is evil, thus they denied Jesus could have come in a human body.

The book of Romans goes on to describe the depravation resulting from rejecting the knowledge of God. The first thing it talks about is idolatry. They took those things which were meant to reveal God, and worshiped them instead.

Romans 1:23 (KJV) And changed the glory of the uncorruptible God into an image made like to corruptible man, and to birds, and fourfooted beasts, and creeping things.

Jesus is the *"image of the invisible God."*[61] How often has religion portrayed an image of God that looks like corruptible man, (created good but defiled by sin) instead of the image of God, revealed in Jesus, the sinless man?

The next thing Romans 1 describes is people who have rejected the knowledge of God, degrading their bodies through sexual immorality. This is the result of rejecting the knowledge of God by rejecting God's creation as evil.

Then the chapter continues to describe the state of people who have traded the truth about God for a lie. Notice it

---

[61] Colossians 1:15

4. An Antichrist Spirit Promotes Sexual Immorality And Violence

again mentions lack of natural affection in the context of sexual immorality. It also uses the word *"unmerciful,"* which denotes the breaking down of natural empathy.

Romans 1:24, 28-31(KJV) Wherefore God also gave them up to uncleanness through the lusts of their own hearts, to dishonour their own bodies between themselves:... And even as they did not like to retain God in their knowledge, God gave them over to a reprobate mind, to do those things which are not convenient; Being filled with all unrighteousness, fornication, wickedness, covetousness, maliciousness; full of envy, murder, debate, deceit, malignity; whisperers, Backbiters, haters of God, despiteful, proud, boasters, inventors of evil things, disobedient to parents, Without understanding, covenant breakers, without natural affection, implacable, unmerciful...

We see the same thing in Paul's letter to Timothy. He wrote about men *"without natural affection,"* who had a *"form of godliness"* and seduced women.

2 Timothy 1:2-3, 5-6 (KJV) For men shall be lovers of their own selves, covetous, boasters, proud, blasphemers, disobedient to parents, unthankful, unholy, Without natural affection...Having a form of godliness, but denying the power thereof: from such turn away. For of this sort are they which creep into houses, and lead captive silly women laden with sins, led away with divers lusts

I mentioned earlier that only a few decades ago, leaders kicked people out of some churches in Brazil for playing soccer. This rejection of natural pleasure as *"sinful"* by the church is a reflection on the influence of an antichrist spirit.

    A pastor got angry at me on my first trip to Brazil. I was playing a lot with the children. I've always made a point of spending time with the children when I'm on a mission trip.

I love children, and I've volunteered at children's homes in several countries.

I learned the pastor thought I must be a pedophile. What?! He imagined I was a pedophile because I think kids are fun and delightful! Our playful romping had nothing to do with sex. I'm a fierce protector of children, not a predator!

Titus 1:15-16 To the pure all things are pure, but to the corrupt and unbelieving nothing is pure. Their very minds and consciences are corrupted. They profess to know God, but they deny him by their actions...

When a person rejects the natural realm as evil, natural affection becomes a bad thing! Children's play is also frowned upon. An antichrist spirit may manifest in the disliking of children. Of course, sometimes children get rowdy at the wrong time and place. However, to many people under an antichrist spirit's influence, there's no right time or place for children's play.

People also took offence when parents brought their children to Jesus. In response, Jesus said *"Let the little children come to me, and don't hinder them."*[62] We see the manifestation of an antichrist spirit in a religious setting when simple, healthy, natural fun is frowned upon. We see it when people discourage healthy natural affection.

I've often observed the abundance of sexual scandals in churches with legalistic teachings about dating and purity. They had a slant against innocent and wholesome things, as if they were evil. This resulted in a proliferation of sexual perversion and covering up sexual scandals. I know people who were personally involved in one of these messes.

My grandparents, decades ago, attended a strict *"Christian"* college. They had an *"18 inch"* rule. Male and female students had to have a distance of eighteen inches between them at all times. Holding hands was a no-no! This

---

[62] Mark 10:14

4. An Antichrist Spirit Promotes Sexual Immorality And Violence

same college today has a reputation as a hotbed of sexual promiscuity.

Sadly, it seems we are always hearing another story of a pastor in Brazil caught sexually abusing others. A week or two ago, we heard of a pastor in my city found raping his own son. Yesterday, I heard the pastor of a church on my street sent a text message of himself naked to all the members of his church. Many of them left. He had intended it for the woman he was having an affair with, but sent it to his church members by mistake.

These kinds of things often happen in churches which have a prudish, Gnostic attitude towards physical affection and enjoyment. They feel stifling. In general, if kids can't stand it, get out! The healthiest churches I have seen are happy places for kids. When people treat pure and holy things as if they were impure, it shows their minds and consciences are defiled.

We see the influence of an antichrist spirit in our societies when everything is sexualized. Kids grow up being taught that normal feelings of affection and love equate to sex. People with defiled minds and consciences consider strong feelings of affection for the same sex to be homosexuality. To the corrupt and unbelieving, nothing is pure.

The truth is that a strong sense of natural affection, both for people of the same gender and of the opposite gender, is healthy and is holy! When your conscience is purified, everything changes! The work of the Holy Spirit in my life has caused me to delight in people, male and female. It has restored and strengthened natural affection!

Natural affection is a godly barrier to sexual immorality, not a cause of it. Kids who receive a good dose of healthy affection when they are young will thrive. A little girl who gets lots of hugs and kisses from her daddy is much less likely to become promiscuous when she is older.

In *Present Access To Heaven* I mention my former relationship with a Russian girlfriend, whom I'd planned to marry. I had strong feelings for her. We held hands and I kissed her on the cheek and on the forehead. Yet it was out of the question for me to try kissing her open-mouthed or doing anything beyond that.

Why? Because I loved her so much. I didn't want to do anything that would hurt her or make her feel bad. I knew it would hurt both of us to become sexually involved outside of marriage. My deep affection for her was a barrier to immorality. That's how it should be when we understand the sanctity of the body.

I was glad to have no have regrets when I met my wife! In the same way, love and affection for my wife made sex before marriage out of the question. I understood the statistics I cited earlier. I knew premarital sex would cause feelings of guilt and regret, and be a destabilizing factor in our relationship.

God's grace has preserved me and protected me from a lot of pain and regret. I'm so glad I encountered the Holy Spirit at a young age. For those who do have regrets about the past, take heart! The blood of Jesus cleanses from all unrighteousness. Jesus is the door out of pain, guilt, and regret, and into heaven now! The Holy Spirit is already working to restore natural affection and all that was lost through sin. Say yes to his work in you!

If you are dealing with physical disease as a result of your past, be whole now! Jesus loves you so much that he not only carried all of your sin on himself, but he suffered carrying your diseases so you wouldn't have to suffer with them. What love! Jesus saw your suffering under the weight of sickness and guilt, and he cried out to God the Father *"Father! Put it on me!"* Your sin and your disease were destroyed with Jesus on the cross. Then he rose again, victorious over sin and disease and all the works of the devil!

Here are some recommended websites for further reading:

www.yourbrainonporn.com
www.fightthenewdrug.org
www.pornharmsresearch.com

4. An Antichrist Spirit Promotes Sexual Immorality And Violence

www.socialcostsofpornography.com
www.nofap.com

5. Re-Sensitization And Undoing The Works Of The Devil

The Incarnation Undoes The Works Of The Devil

In the last chapter, we examined how an antichrist spirit desensitizes people with its lies. Just as the devil is always working to desensitize people, the Holy Spirit is constantly working to re-sensitize people. The work of the Holy Spirit restores the natural affection and the humanness of humanity. Jesus came to undo the work of the devil!

1 John 3:8 (JUB) For this purpose the Son of God appeared, that he might undo the works of the devil.

As we see in *Present Access To Heaven,* the gospel re-sensitizes us, frees us from guilt and shame, and empowers us to love like God loves. All the issues mentioned in the last chapter are tangible problems. The incarnation demonstrates a gospel with tangible results; it has the power to restore every aspect of our being.

If we don't see tangible results, we should consider whether we believe the authentic gospel or a message resembling the gospel but altering its core truths. A weakened form of the gospel acknowledges the incarnation but denies what it implies. This is like an inoculation, a half-truth, which, in the hands of the enemy, is concocted to make us resistant to the real thing.

The lie of a spirit denying the incarnation is at the root of all of the problems in our society. The truth that Jesus came in the flesh reaches just as far, stopping destruction in its tracks and undoing the worst of messes.

Healing And Spiritual Warfare

Few books on spiritual warfare focus primarily on healing and ministering to people's physical needs. Yet much of the focus of Jesus' earthly ministry was healing the sick. In fact, the gospels talk more about Jesus healing the sick than they do about being born again! It was after Jesus' disciples healed many sick people and cast out many demons that he said *"I watched Satan fall from heaven like a flash of lightning."*[63]

Matthew 9:35 Jesus went about all the cities and villages, teaching in their synagogues, and proclaiming the good news of the kingdom, and curing every disease and every sickness.

The healing ministry demonstrates everything an antichrist spirit denies. It demonstrates that the body is holy. It shows that God isn't far away and mysterious, but is with us. It testifies that the gospel isn't just a theory but is tangible. It demonstrates that God has chosen to put his Holy Spirit in human bodies, and that the Spirit of Christ is in the church.

The healing ministry strikes at the root of sexual immorality, violence, drug abuse, poverty, and crime. Just as watching graphic violence desensitizes people, seeing God's power touch people's bodies re-sensitizes them, undoing the work of the devil.

I've seen so many people weep when God's power touched their bodies. I've also wept upon seeing people healed or having flashbacks of healing. Something more than physical healing happens. The Holy Spirit softens people's hearts. We demonstrate that Jesus has come in the flesh.

In *Present Access To Heaven* I mention whole families tangibly feeling the weight of God's glory. Several people were healed, and sometimes others felt shivers of God's power going through their bodies. Some wept. What kind of effect can we expect from this? We should expect the redemptive

---

[63] Luke 10:18

5. Re-Sensitization And Undoing The Works Of The Devil

effects of re-sensitization to be just as far-reaching as the destructive effects of desensitization.

Seeing the effects of the Holy Spirit on the human body is beautiful. Pornography degrades humanity, treating human bodies as common objects, separated from the soul. The Holy Spirit exults humanity, joining us to God and making us participants in his nature. Seeing human faces shining with God's glory is the opposite of viewing pornography.

When we see emotional reactions to healing ministry, like weeping or joy, it's because empathy and natural affection are being restored. By demonstrating the sanctity of the body we strike at the heart of the spirit of lust, the spirit of violence, the spirit of addiction, and every other evil spirit which breaks up relationships and destroys people's bodies.

An Infection Under The Tongue

I remember an evening church service after I'd started practicing words of knowledge. I felt like God showed me a few things, so I talked to the pastor. He gave me a chance to share.

One of the things I said was *"I feel like there's someone here who has an infection underneath your tongue. If that's you, Jesus is healing you."* I had never heard of an infection under the tongue, and this seemed like a strange thing to say. I wasn't sure if it was just a crazy thought which popped into my head, or if I was really hearing the Holy Spirit.

Later, I found out there was a young teenager visiting that evening. She had tried to pierce her tongue. In the process she hurt herself, and her tongue got infected. After it got better she tried again, and it got infected again! When I said I believed someone had an infection under the tongue, she said to her friend *"How does he know that?"* God healed her tongue!

I don't have a problem with body piercing itself. Yet when a girl pulls out her own tongue and stabs it, (and does the same thing again after it didn't work the first time) it seems to me that a spirit of self-harm is involved.

I don't know anything about her life after God healed her tongue. I do know that what happened was about much more than healing her tongue. It was striking the spirit of self-harm which led her into destructive behavior.

I have a friend who was once addicted to cutting herself. Cutting is a big problem among many youth. They feel release when they bleed. There's a chemical dependence aspect to self-harm. When people cut, the brain releases chemicals which give them a high feeling.

Jesus came in the flesh, and men cut his physical body with a whip. He carried our shame. Jesus' body was cut to deliver us from cutting and self-harm.

My friend had scars all over her arms. She gave her life to the Lord and soon got free from the addiction to cutting. The Lord did a marvelous work in her life! Some time after she had quit cutting, the Lord miraculously removed many of her scars! He took away even the reminders of her old life.

I've heard testimonies of others whose scars dissolved and they were simultaneously delivered from cutting addictions. We can expect people to be physically healed and to simultaneously be set free from all kinds of self-destructive behaviors.

Delivered From Alcoholism When She Realized God Healed Her!

I heard Dan Mohler share this story shortly after I first met him. It stands out as a great example to illustrate how ministering healing softens people's hearts and has long-reaching effects beyond just the healing of the physical problem.

A woman had stage four cancer. The doctors only gave her a short time to live. Dan laid his hands on her and commanded the cancer to leave. Although she attended church, she was a secret alcoholic. When she met Dan she was miserable, bitter and angry. She was angry at God because she was dying of cancer, and angry at people who had hurt her.

She continued to mope and drink away her sorrows for six weeks after Dan laid his hands on her, angry at God and

5. Re-Sensitization And Undoing The Works Of The Devil

expecting to die. Then she went to the doctors and they didn't find a trace of cancer in her body! She wept, realizing how wrong she had been to blame God for her suffering. At the same time she lost all desire for alcohol and had no withdrawal symptoms. God had healed her when she was still his enemy, still angry, bitter, and full of unforgiveness!

She was in this state for six weeks after she was healed, but when she realized what God had done for her, she was set free from alcoholism and from the bitterness in her heart. The healing revealed God's heart to her. It demonstrated the value of her body to God. It showed her that Jesus has come in the flesh.

Seeing violence against people on TV makes my stomach turn. It disturbs me as if I were a child again, because seeing God heal people has re-wired my brain. I've been re-sensitized. Viewing the work of the Holy Spirit healing people has the very opposite effect as viewing pornography and violence.

I don't know that from studies or statistics. I don't think scientists have done any scientific studies about the changes taking place in a person's brain as they behold the work of the Holy Spirit. But I know it from experience.

In chapter 10 you'll read the story of my first time helping a man in a wheelchair get up and walk. It impacted my emotions so much that the picture of the joy on his face after walking etched itself in my mind, and I often weep years later when I tell the story. I'm sure this experience created new neural pathways in my brain, affecting my perceptions and responses to whatever inputs my mind receives.

When the Holy Spirit re-sensitizes us, things we'd become accustomed to and even attracted to now become grievous. Lust becomes repulsive, but natural affection is restored. When we are desensitized, people seem ugly to us. When we are re-sensitized, all kinds of people become beautiful and delightful. Our perceptions change.

Meeting Physical Needs

Just as healing does, meeting people's physical needs demonstrates Jesus has come in the flesh. It makes God tangible. Demonstrating acts of compassion and kindness has the same effect as healing the sick. It re-sensitizes. It can change the structure of people's brains.

Sometimes the physical need is for food, water, or shelter. Jesus multiplied food when the crowds were hungry. Sometimes the need is for a mother and father, or for healthy friendships and natural affection. Jesus welcomed little children and blessed them. He made sure his mother would be cared for as he was dying.

John 19:26-27 When Jesus saw his mother and the disciple whom he loved standing beside her, he said to his mother, "Woman, here is your son." Then he said to the disciple, "Here is your mother." And from that hour the disciple took her into his own home.

Psalm 68:5-6 (NIV) A father to the fatherless, a defender of widows, is God in his holy dwelling. God sets the lonely in families, he leads out the prisoners with singing.

I know from experience how much of a difference a father can make. When I was in fourth grade, my dad worked third shift to try to make ends meet. I hated school. Most of the kids there were mean to me. I was angry and miserable, and had fits of rage. I also shoplifted and stole money from my parents.

My mom and dad were worried about me. My behavior had deteriorated to the point that they didn't know how to handle me.

My parents talked with my grandmother and said *"What should we do?"* She gave them some wise advice. *"Why don't you see if Jan can pick him up from school during the lunch break and spend some time with him? He needs more time with his dad."*

5. Re-Sensitization And Undoing The Works Of The Devil

So they arranged with the school for me to spend lunch and recess with my father. I loved it! It was a big relief to get away from the school for an hour. I hadn't realized how much I missed my dad. It especially meant a lot to me when my dad took me out to eat and bought me a sub. We lived on a shoestring budget and rarely went out to eat, so this was something really special.

I stopped taking money from my dad's wallet, and my behavior improved. I was still technically stealing from him, since he was the breadwinner and I continued to sneak money from my mom's purse, but it was an emotional decision, not a rational one. I felt like I loved my dad too much to take money from his wallet.

My own experience has inspired me. I know what it's like to be a child feeling caught in the middle of everything and needing love and attention. I've regularly volunteered to work with children in the United States and in several other countries. I pray the love of God manifested through me would have an effect in the lives of children that's as far-reaching as the damage done by fatherlessness.

Earlier, I mentioned the prevalence of sexual infidelity and the epidemic of fatherlessness in Russia. Most Russian orphans get involved in prostitution, drugs, and organized crime, ending up homeless or in prison. Over 10% commit suicide within the first year of leaving the orphanage. The average life expectancy for a Russian orphan is less than 30 years old. Only about a tenth of Russian orphans go on to become functional members of society.[64]

As I studied the Russian language, I watched a Russian film about an orphan. It broke my heart. I prayed *"God, I want to do everything possible to change this."* Facing the facts challenged me to grow in faith and believe for the impossible.

---

[64] Several reputable sites give similar statistics. These include
http://change30.org/about/ and http://howtohelporphans.org/bythenumbers.html
The author was unable to find the original sources for the numbers, some of which were stated to be from Russian sources.

Jesus Has Come In The Flesh

Some people think my faith in God's will to heal and do miracles is an escape from reality. Nothing could be further from the truth. What I believe challenges me to face reality and do something about it. It would be much easier to just believe I can't do anything about the suffering I see, and so hide from it.

I remember visiting kids in Russian children's homes. At one place, I carried three kids at all times, a little boy in each arm and one hanging off of my back. They were dying for attention!

At another children's home in Russia, I remember playing with a little girl, about six years old. I walked all around with her on my shoulders. When I gave the other kids rides as well, she lay on the ground, crying, but she laughed when I came back to her. I can still see her beautiful face, with blond hair and blue eyes. I've prayed for her ever since.

I wished I could do more for these kids than just my short visits. I prayed that God would super-charge the time I had with them. I prayed a seed of love would be planted which would help them to make good decisions and succeed in their futures. I prayed God would connect them in long-term relationships with other people who would help them.

I volunteered with a different type of children's home in Ukraine. Unlike the state-run children's homes in Russia, this was not an orphanage. It was a big family. The founders are American missionaries who rescue children from situations of horrendous abuse and neglect. Their organization is called *"Joshua House Life Centers."*[65] They take in kids as their own children, giving them plenty of love and affection. They pray for them, believe in them, and give them good experiences to replace the horrible memories of the past.

They've saved the lives of these children. Many of them would probably have been dead before the age of 30 if nobody had rescued them. Instead, they're thriving! They have stopped vicious cycles of fatherlessness, crime, and addiction. Their work will affect generations to come.

---

[65] Online. http://joshuahouselifecenters.org/

5. Re-Sensitization And Undoing The Works Of The Devil

Children need love, affection, safety, and security. Those who hold abandoned babies and give attention to hurting children are doing spiritual warfare. They are destroying the work of the devil. Whenever I'm with children, whether they have backgrounds of abuse or have loving parents, I pray my influence will help them to thrive and to make healthy choices in the future. I believe the power of life and death is in my tongue,[66] so I constantly bless them.

Of course, children who have no parents need adoption. They need adults who will make a long-term commitment to love and care for them. Yet even when time is limited, as my time with Russian orphans was, God's love can make its mark on a child's life. It could be the difference between life and death.

This reminds me of an experiment I read about several years ago. I was unable to re-locate the source. Troubled teenagers exhibiting problematic behavior in school were given a short shoulder massage every day before school started. Their behavior improved significantly and their moods became more positive.

Even little things like a shoulder rub for a teenager, or listening to a little girl tell you about the picture she is drawing, can make a big difference. When you buy a meal for a person, it could be the first in a long time that they felt like somebody cared about them. It can impart hope.

My Grandmother worked for many years as the receptionist at a Christian rescue mission, which shelters and feeds the homeless. She took the information of applicants, found out about their needs, and oriented them. Once, as she welcomed a new resident, she said *"You know, this is a Christian mission. I hope while you're here, you'll take the opportunity to read the Bible and find out what God might want for your life."*

The man pulled out a big knife. She was afraid. Rapists and felons had often passed through the mission, but she felt

---
[66] Proverbs 18:21

Jesus Has Come In The Flesh

like the Holy Spirit told her to stay calm. She asked *"What's that knife for?"*

The man said *"I was planning to kill myself with this knife. Nobody has ever cared about me. I just decided not to kill myself, because you're the first person who has ever shown they care about me."* He gave her the knife.

This story isn't unique. I've heard many stories of suicides that have been prevented by a smile or a few friendly words.

Jesus has come in the flesh. If you are born again, he has also come in your flesh. He has put his Spirit in your body so you can reveal his love to the world.

6. The Incarnation Means We Can Touch God

The Word We Have Touched With Our Hands

Throughout this series of books, I've written about tangibly feeling God's presence in my body. These experiences were often triggered by singing praise to the Lord or meditating on scripture. Such experiences are precious to me, because I feel like I have touched God. They remind me of the words of the Apostle John, who emphasized the incarnation more than any other Bible writer.

1 John 1:1-3 We declare to you what was from the beginning, what we have heard, what we have seen with our eyes, what we have looked at and touched with our hands, concerning the word of life— this life was revealed, and we have seen it and testify to it, and declare to you the eternal life that was with the Father and was revealed to us— we declare to you what we have seen and heard so that you also may have fellowship with us; and truly our fellowship is with the Father and with his Son Jesus Christ.

John wasn't talking about a mere theory. He had touched God's word. He had touched Jesus. God's word became tangible when Jesus came in the flesh.

John 1:14 And the Word became flesh and lived among us, and we have seen his glory, the glory as of a father's only son, full of grace and truth.

Jesus Has Come In The Flesh

Luke 24:36-40 While they were talking about this, Jesus himself stood among them and said to them, "Peace be with you." They were startled and terrified, and thought that they were seeing a ghost. He said to them, "Why are you frightened, and why do doubts arise in your hearts? Look at my hands and my feet; see that it is I myself. Touch me and see; for a ghost does not have flesh and bones as you see that I have." And when he had said this, he showed them his hands and his feet.

As a child, I told my friends *"I felt God's hand in my back"* after the Lord healed me. The healing ministry demonstrates every aspect of the incarnation. People often physically feel God's power in their bodies when they're healed. Some people feel heat or electricity. Others feel a hand touching them, parts of their body moving, or something else. These experiences demonstrate that God's word is real and tangible!

I've become accustomed to touching God. Like the apostle John, I have confidence that when I tell people about Jesus I speak of what I have seen and heard, and what my own hands have touched.

Our faith, of course, should rest on God's word and not on what we feel naturally. We shouldn't have to feel God's presence to know God is with us. God's word is truth, whether we feel it or not. Physically sensing God's presence has taught me that God's glory is here and his word is true even when I don't feel like it is. I realized the love of God I was experiencing had always been there, but I simply needed to become aware of it.

In fact, meditating on scriptural truth and being convinced of God's word regardless of feelings triggered most of these tangible experiences. Throughout the writing of this series, I've repeatedly felt the weight of God's glory touch my body as I meditate on scripture's promises and write of Christ's atonement, his resurrection, and the incarnation.

These experiences aren't the basis of my faith, but they are an important part of it. They are also the result of it. Remembering powerful, physical experiences with God's

6. The Incarnation Means We Can Touch God

glory encourages me when I face difficulties and challenges. It reminds me that God's word is powerful and his promises have substance, regardless of my circumstances or what I feel at the moment.

God Is With Us!

The prophet Isaiah prophesied the incarnation about seven-hundred years before it happened! Isaiah said Jesus' name would be *"Immanuel."*

Isaiah 7:14 (AMP) Therefore the Lord Himself will give you a sign: Listen carefully, the virgin will conceive and give birth to a son, and she will call his name Immanuel (God with us).

Immanuel means *"God with us."* The Spirit of God in a human body is God with us. When Jesus came with a human body, he revealed God. God was no longer far away, un-knowable, or mysterious.

Job wished God was a man so he could approach him face to face. God seemed so far, distant, and unreachable to Job. He was terrified of God.

Job 9:32 (NKJV) "For He is not a man, as I am, That I may answer Him, And that we should go to court together. Nor is there any mediator between us, Who may lay his hand on us both. Let Him take His rod away from me, And do not let dread of Him terrify me. Then I would speak and not fear Him, But it is not so with me.

God answered the cry of Job's heart. He came as a man! Because Jesus came in the flesh, we can approach God face to face. We can see him as he is. Everything Job needed was provided in Christ. Job wanted a mediator and Jesus is the mediator between us and the Father. Jesus removed the rod from us as he died on the cross, carrying our sins, pains, and diseases. Jesus revealed the loving heart of the Father. We need

Jesus Has Come In The Flesh

no longer be terrified by the dread of God! We can touch God and know him, because Jesus came in the flesh.

Because antichrist denies the incarnation, it denies God is with us. An antichrist spirit says God is far off; un-reachable. It teaches people to pray and speak as if God is far away. This is one of the standards by which we can judge any spirit and any teaching. Does it acknowledge God is with us, or does it say he is far away?

We can also recognize when an antichrist spirit is lying to us personally. It opposes the anointing by getting us to doubt God is with us. It says God has abandoned us. If a voice in your head is telling you God has abandoned you, tell it to shut up now! It's not you. It's a lying spirit. Refuse to accept the lies of a spirit that denies Jesus has come in the flesh. God is with us!

I remember a church I visited where I saw one person after another healed. As I stood there, praying for people and watching the Holy Spirit touch them, I couldn't stop weeping. The feeling Jesus himself was standing beside me overwhelmed me. I remembered the last words of Christ that Matthew records before his ascension.

Matthew 28:20 And remember, I am with you always...

Why did it feel like Jesus was standing beside me? The awareness of Jesus' loving-kindness and goodness as people were healed overwhelmed me. Many people feel like God is far away. The healing ministry demonstrates that God is with us. The manifestation of Christ's healing in our mortal bodies shows people God is here, and they can reach out and touch him.

I mentioned earlier how Gnosticism influenced Augustine and other early church fathers. Neo-Platonism also heavily influenced them. One of the ideas of Neo-Platonism is that God is completely inaccessible to human beings.[67] A

---

[67] The Perennial Tradition of Neoplatonism, p. 188–194

6. The Incarnation Means We Can Touch God

system of thought claiming God is inaccessible denies that God is with us, thus denying Jesus came in the flesh.

Every spirit that denies Jesus has come in the flesh is antichrist. An antichrist influence came into the teaching of these early church fathers through Neo-Platonism. This is not to say they themselves were antichrists. Although they acknowledged the fact Jesus came in the flesh, there were ways they thought and taught as if he hadn't.

Giving People A Sign

As I touched God's glory with increasing frequency, I learned I could show people a sign to share the gospel with them. I have them hold their hands out, and pray they physically feel the weight of God's glory. Many people feel something tangibly in their hands. Some people don't feel the weight, but feel heat or electricity.

I've often used this demonstration to explain that we can touch God, because Jesus came as a man. I quote the apostle John, who spoke of the Word he touched with his hands. I explain that God's word isn't just a theory but is powerful. God's goodness is so real that it has substance, and we can feel its weight. I also explain that the things I do are possible for me because I've been cleansed from sin by the blood of Jesus and I have full access to God through him.

If the person doesn't feel anything, I don't over-analyze why. It doesn't mean anything is wrong with them. Often, people who feel nothing the first time later feel God's presence in a powerful and tangible way. Sometimes I don't even have people hold out their hands. They feel the weight of God's glory on their whole bodies as I speak or pray. These signs demonstrate that Jesus has come in the flesh, God is with us, and God is accessible. They touch people's hearts and draw them to the Lord.

Offer Your Body To The Lord

When we understand that salvation is for our whole being, including our bodies, we discover that giving our lives to the Lord includes dedicating our bodies to him.

Romans 12:1-2 (NIV) Therefore, I urge you, brothers and sisters, in view of God's mercy, to offer your bodies as a living sacrifice, holy and pleasing to God—this is your true and proper worship. Do not conform to the pattern of this world, but be transformed by the renewing of your mind. Then you will be able to test and approve what God's will is—his good, pleasing and perfect will.

When I feel the presence of God in my body, it shows me my body is special to God. As I feel my body vibrating with the love of God, I pray with tears *"God, take every part of my body! I yield it to you. I give every part of my being to you."*

I've become increasingly aware of the presence of God in my body. My body is the temple of the Holy Spirit. These hands are Jesus' hands. When I touch someone, it is as if Jesus were touching them. When I work, it is unto the Lord.

These feet are Jesus' feet, dedicated to bringing the good news of the gospel to others. My eyes are His eyes, looking on people with purity and a love that pierces the soul. They see what Jesus sees. My arms are his arms. When they carry children, it is Jesus who is holding them. My mouth is his mouth. May it only speak his words, bringing life to others.

Ephesians 4:29 Let no evil talk come out of your mouths, but only what is useful for building up, as there is need, so that your words may give grace to those who hear.

Romans 6:19 For just as you once presented your members as slaves to impurity and to greater and greater iniquity, so now present your members as slaves to righteousness for sanctification.

6. The Incarnation Means We Can Touch God

When I respond to God's touch by yielding my body to him, I bear the fruit of righteousness and purity. When I minister to others and they feel God's presence touch their bodies, I know God is drawing them to present the members of their bodies to the Lord as slaves to righteousness.

1 Thessalonians 4:1-8 Finally, brothers and sisters, we ask and urge you in the Lord Jesus that, as you learned from us how you ought to live and to please God (as, in fact, you are doing), you should do so more and more. For you know what instructions we gave you through the Lord Jesus. For this is the will of God, your sanctification: that you abstain from fornication; that each one of you know how to control your own body in holiness and honor, not with lustful passion, like the Gentiles who do not know God; that no one wrong or exploit a brother or sister in this matter, because the Lord is an avenger in all these things, just as we have already told you beforehand and solemnly warned you. For God did not call us to impurity but in holiness. Therefore whoever rejects this rejects not human authority but God, who also gives his Holy Spirit to you.

As I yield my body to the Lord, I become increasingly aware that my body is his temple. I'm conscious of the Spirit of Christ dwelling in me and giving life to my mortal body.

Romans 8:11 If the Spirit of him who raised Jesus from the dead dwells in you, he who raised Christ from the dead will give life to your mortal bodies also through his Spirit that dwells in you.

7. Why Did Jesus Have To Come As A Man?
Man's Authority
In the creation account in Genesis 1, we repeatedly read that God saw what he had created was good. Finally we get to the creation of man.

Genesis 1:26-28,31 Then God said, "Let us make humankind in our image, according to our likeness; and let them have dominion over the fish of the sea, and over the birds of the air, and over the cattle, and over all the wild animals of the earth, and over every creeping thing that creeps upon the earth."

So God created humankind in his image, in the image of God he created them; male and female he created them.

God blessed them, and God said to them, "Be fruitful and multiply, and fill the earth and subdue it; and have dominion over the fish of the sea and over the birds of the air and over every living thing that moves upon the earth."

...God saw everything that he had made, and indeed, it was very good.

Before God created man, he saw that what he had made was good. After creating man, he said it was very good. Every other part of creation expressed some aspect of God's nature, but man was created in God's image. Man was the highest order of creation.

God delighted in mankind. He still does. Throughout scripture, we see God's desire for relationship and partnership with humanity. Again and again, God chose human beings to partner with him in accomplishing his will. God looked for men and women such as Noah, Joseph, Moses, Deborah Esther, Ruth, King David, Isaiah, Mary, Paul, Priscilla and countless others.

Psalm 147:11 ...the LORD takes pleasure in those who fear him, in those who hope in his steadfast love.

2 Chronicles 16:9 (RSV) For the eyes of the LORD run to and fro throughout the whole earth, to show his might on behalf of those whose heart is blameless toward him.

God could have chosen to control every detail of everything that happened. But he chose not to. He wanted mankind to share in his work, so he gave authority to men and women. God's intention from the beginning was that people in right relationship with him would extend his dominion on earth.

Psalm 8:3-6 When I look at your heavens, the work of your fingers, the moon and the stars that you have established; what are human beings that you are mindful of them, mortals that you care for them?
    Yet you have made them a little lower than God, and crowned them with glory and honor. You have given them dominion over the works of your hands; you have put all things under their feet

Psalm 115:16 The heavens are the LORD's heavens, but the earth he has given to human beings.

John Wesley said *"God does nothing except in response to believing prayer."* Another time he said *"It seems God is limited by our prayer life — that He can do nothing for humanity unless someone asks him."* Scripture says something similar.

Amos 3:7 Surely the Lord GOD does nothing, without revealing his secret to his servants the prophets.

7. Why Did Jesus Have To Come As A Man?

There was a problem after the fall. Although some people sought the Lord, there was no one without sin. Even the best of men had become perverted through sin.

Romans 3:9-18 ...all, both Jews and Greeks, are under the power of sin, as it is written:
"There is no one who is righteous, not even one; there is no one who has understanding, there is no one who seeks God. All have turned aside, together they have become worthless; there is no one who shows kindness, there is not even one."
"Their throats are opened graves; they use their tongues to deceive." "The venom of vipers is under their lips." "Their mouths are full of cursing and bitterness." "Their feet are swift to shed blood; ruin and misery are in their paths, and the way of peace they have not known." "There is no fear of God before their eyes."

Romans 3:23 All have sinned and fall short of the glory of God

God gave authority to humans, and he searched for a righteous person to partner with him. His purpose was always that mankind in right relationship with him would exercise his dominion— heaven's dominion— on the earth. However, God didn't find anyone who was righteous. Men and women still partnered with God to a certain extent, but it was always limited because of sin. God needed a sinless human being.

Ezekiel 22:29-31 The people of the land have practiced extortion and committed robbery; they have oppressed the poor and needy, and have extorted from the sojourner without redress. And I sought for a man among them who should build up the wall and stand in the breach before me for the land, that I should not destroy it; but I found none. Therefore I have poured out my indignation upon them; I have consumed them with the fire of my wrath; their way have I requited upon their heads, says the Lord GOD."

Ezekiel described God's search for a sinless man who could stand in the gap. He wanted to show mercy, but he couldn't do it because he needed a man to agree with him! Yet he found no man that was righteous.

I'm not suggesting God isn't omnipotent. Is God limited? Only by the limitations he places on himself. By delegating authority over the earth to mankind and choosing not to rescind it, God has limited himself. Instead of rescinding man's authority, God chose to redeem man. In a sense, God has chosen to need us.

Some may think *"How dare you say God couldn't do something!"* Well, there's one thing scripture says God can't do. He can't go against his own word. He can't lie.[68] To have decided to take control regardless of humanity, he would have had to withdraw the dominion he gave to human beings and to give up on his purpose for mankind — of co-laboring with him. Instead, he had a redemptive plan.

Isaiah chapter 59 describes the same dilemma. We just read part of it, since it's quoted in Romans 3. For the sake of brevity, I've selected some of the key verses. The chapter starts by potently describing the anguish and separation from God that sin causes. Then it again describes God finding no righteous person to intervene. The conclusion? He stretched out his own arm.

Isaiah 59:8-9, 11-12, 14-17, 20 (RSV) The way of peace they know not, and there is no justice in their paths; they have made their roads crooked, no one who goes in them knows peace. Therefore justice is far from us, and righteousness does not overtake us; we look for light, and behold, darkness, and for brightness, but we walk in gloom.

---

[68] Numbers 23:19, 1 Samuel 15:29, Hebrews 6:18

7. Why Did Jesus Have To Come As A Man?

...we look for justice, but there is none; for salvation, but it is far from us. For our transgressions are multiplied before thee, and our sins testify against us;

Justice is turned back, and righteousness stands afar off; for truth has fallen in the public squares, and uprightness cannot enter. Truth is lacking, and he who departs from evil makes himself a prey.

The LORD saw it, and it displeased him that there was no justice. He saw that there was no man, and wondered that there was no one to intervene; then his own arm brought him victory, and his righteousness upheld him. He put on righteousness as a breastplate, and a helmet of salvation upon his head...

"And he will come to Zion as Redeemer, to those in Jacob who turn from transgression, says the LORD.

Again, God needed a righteous person, but he couldn't find one. So his own arm brought him victory, and his righteousness upheld him. How did God stretch out his arm? When God saw that there was no righteous man, he came as a man. Jesus came in the flesh.

God never abandoned his purpose of extending his dominion on earth through humans in right relationship with him. He never gave up on his plan for mankind!

Psalm 33:11 (NIV) But the plans of the LORD stand firm forever, the purposes of his heart through all generations.

One of the primary scriptural reasons Jesus had to come in the flesh is this: Jesus had to come in the flesh because God gave authority to men, but no man was righteous. Mankind misused that authority and brought death and destruction. They partnered with Satan instead of with God, and they became corrupt.

It's always been mankind that's had authority on earth. God's will is done as human beings partner with him. Satan can do nothing on this earth if he doesn't find some way to get man's agreement with him.

Romans 5 describes how death came through man and also how redemption comes through man. We already looked at part of this passage in *Present Access To Heaven*. Let's go back to it now and see how it relates to Jesus coming in the flesh.

Romans 5:12-21 Therefore, just as sin came into the world through one man, and death came through sin, and so death spread to all because all have sinned— sin was indeed in the world before the law, but sin is not reckoned when there is no law.

Yet death exercised dominion from Adam to Moses, even over those whose sins were not like the transgression of Adam, who is a type of the one who was to come. But the free gift is not like the trespass. For if the many died through the one man's trespass, much more surely have the grace of God and the free gift in the grace of the one man, Jesus Christ, abounded for the many. And the free gift is not like the effect of the one man's sin. For the judgment following one trespass brought condemnation, but the free gift following many trespasses brings justification.

If, because of the one man's trespass, death exercised dominion through that one, much more surely will those who receive the abundance of grace and the free gift of righteousness exercise dominion in life through the one man, Jesus Christ. Therefore just as one man's trespass led to condemnation for all, so one man's act of righteousness leads to justification and life for all. For just as by the one man's disobedience the many were made sinners, so by the one man's obedience the many will be made righteous.

Romans chapter five is clear. Death exercised dominion through sinful man. Life exercises dominion through Jesus, the righteous man. Romans 5 extends the truth of the incarnation by teaching that people who have been cleansed from sin by

7. Why Did Jesus Have To Come As A Man?

Christ's blood and made righteous will also exercise dominion in life through Jesus.

Jesus had to come in the flesh because God gave dominion to human beings. Because Jesus came in the flesh and freed us from sin, we can now exercise dominion in life. God's kingdom can now be established in this earth-realm, because once again righteous, sinless men and women walk the earth! As I have often quoted, Jesus was the firstborn among many brothers![69]

We see in *Present Access To Heaven* that heaven is heaven because God is there. The Spirit of God in human bodies is heaven on earth! Jesus not only came in the flesh, but he has come in our flesh! Paul said it so well in his letter to the Colossians:

Colossians 1:27 To them God chose to make known how great among the Gentiles are the riches of the glory of this mystery, which is Christ in you, the hope of glory.

Jesus Demonstrated The Authority God Gave Man By Coming As A Man

Some of the scribes said Jesus was blaspheming because he forgave sins. They had no problem with the idea that God could forgive sins, but they were offended at the idea that a man could. Yet Jesus said their thoughts were evil.

Matthew 9:1-8 And after getting into a boat he crossed the sea and came to his own town. And just then some people were carrying a paralyzed man lying on a bed. When Jesus saw their faith, he said to the paralytic, "Take heart, son; your sins are forgiven."

Then some of the scribes said to themselves, "This man is blaspheming." But Jesus, perceiving their thoughts, said, "Why do you think evil in your hearts? For which is easier, to say, 'Your sins are forgiven,' or to say, 'Stand up and walk'?

---
[69] Romans 8:29

But so that you may know that the Son of Man has authority on earth to forgive sins"—he then said to the paralytic—"Stand up, take your bed and go to your home." And he stood up and went to his home. When the crowds saw it, they were filled with awe, and they glorified God, who had given such authority to human beings.

Jesus, coming as a man, showed us the authority God gave to mankind. When that authority was questioned, he demonstrated it by healing. The point of Jesus' miracle was not just to reveal that God is powerful. The people already believed God was powerful, but he was far-off to them. Jesus showed them God had given authority to human beings. That was why they glorified God.

That was what God always wanted. He wanted to be glorified in mankind, and to glorify mankind with himself. God has given us the privilege of doing his work and sharing in his glory! Later, Jesus confirmed to his disciples that the power to forgive was theirs.

John 20:23 If you forgive the sins of any, they are forgiven them; if you retain the sins of any, they are retained.

The Antichrist Spirit Denies The Authority God Gave To Man

Because the antichrist spirit denies Jesus came in the flesh, it denies there was any need for Jesus to come as a man. The antichrist spirit denies the authority God gave to humanity over the creation. It opposes God's eternal purpose of mankind exercising authority on earth and extending his dominion through right relationship with him.

If God controlled everything, Jesus didn't need to come in the flesh! And if you have nothing to do with whether or not God's will is accomplished, why would he have put his Spirit in your body?

Our *"hope of glory"* is the fact that Christ is in us, God has revealed his will to us, and he is able to accomplish it

7. Why Did Jesus Have To Come As A Man?

through us! An antichrist spirit says God controls everything and doesn't need men, because it denies Jesus came as a man and denies the Spirit of Christ dwells in you. It denies that the church is the *"body of Christ."*

If we are the body of Christ, God needs us to accomplish his purposes on the earth. The way he's chosen to work isn't from somewhere up in the sky, but through you and I.[70] God has revealed his will to you, and he wants to accomplish it through you!

If the antichrist spirit can convince us that God doesn't need us, we won't do the things God told us to do. We won't heal the sick, cast out demons, or set the captives free. We won't be able to stand in faith or persevere. If we have nothing to do with whether or not God's will happens, there's not much point to the scriptural commands to pray, to believe, to preach the gospel, or do anything else. The antichrist opposes the anointing by denying the incarnation.

The anointing is the Spirit of God in man. It's Jesus come in the flesh, and it's Jesus come in our flesh. If we don't do our part, not much will happen. Do you want to see God move? Then act. The Holy Spirit is always working. He's waiting eagerly for you to partner with him! Add your *"amen"* to God's *"yes."* When I see a person in need, I know the Holy Spirit is working. I need to do my part and partner with him.

That's what God has always wanted! It's a wonderful privilege that we have to co-labor with God! It's a love relationship. God is like a father building a treehouse with his son. The father could do everything himself, but he loves that little boy! He wants to work together with him.

I'm in awe of this privilege God has given me, that I should be called a son of God. I love my Father with all my heart. I pray each one reading this would come to a realization of the wonderful joy of partnering with the Heavenly Father and sharing in his love and nature.

---

[70] Yeah, I know this is bad grammar, but I like the way it sounds!

Jesus Has Come In The Flesh

1 John 3:1 (KJV) Behold, what manner of love the Father hath bestowed upon us, that we should be called the sons of God

Throughout scripture, we see God desiring to partner with human beings. God does his part, and we do our part. When we understand God's purpose and his plans for mankind, our hearts will overflow with thanksgiving to him. He is wonderful, he is perfect, and his ways are perfect.

What Is Satan Afraid Of?

Satan isn't nearly as opposed to people believing in God's existence and power as he is opposed to people understanding they can know God's will and see what he is like through Christ. Satan doesn't seem to feel threatened when people believe there's a God up there in the sky. However, he's terrified of Christians finding out that Christ lives in them! He doesn't mind our religious activities as long as he can get us to keep asking God to do everything for us, yet failing to do our part to partner with the Holy Spirit.

    I regularly hear people pray *"God, please rebuke all evil."* Where did God ever tell us to ask him to rebuke evil? He told us to rebuke it. Many Christians are crippled, resulting in powerlessness, because they're acting and speaking as if Jesus doesn't live in them. Believers need to learn to use their God-given authority.

When Not To Cry Out To God

(This section is partly inspired by a John G. Lake sermon on Moses' prayer,[71] and partly by a message I heard Bill Johnson share about Jesus in the boat with his disciples.)

Is there ever a time when we should not cry out to God? Consider the following stories from scripture.

---

[71] Lake, John G., and Roberts Liardon. *"Moses' Rebuke."* John G. Lake: The Complete Collection of His Life Teachings. New Kensington, PA: Whitaker House, 2004. 874. Print.

7. Why Did Jesus Have To Come As A Man?

In Exodus 14, we read the story of the Israelites trapped between the Red Sea and the Egyptian army. It was a desperate situation with no hope from a natural perspective. The Israelites quickly forgot the supernatural things the Lord had already done to deliver them. They were grumbling and complaining to Moses.

Then Moses prayed, asking God for deliverance. This seems like a spiritual, mature response to the situation, doesn't it? However, God said something to Moses that's a little surprising.

Exodus 14:15-17 Then the Lord said to Moses, "Why do you cry out to me? Tell the Israelites to go forward. But you lift up your staff, and stretch out your hand over the sea and divide it, that the Israelites may go into the sea on dry ground. Then I will harden the hearts of the Egyptians so that they will go in after them; and so I will gain glory for myself over Pharaoh and all his army, his chariots, and his chariot drivers.

The Lord asked Moses *"Why do you cry out to me?"* Crying out to the Lord wasn't the appropriate response. Moses already had God's word. The Lord had commissioned him to deliver the Israelites.

The staff represents authority. Moses was to use his authority to divide the sea, not ask God to do it. God would do his part and accomplish a great victory.

We have a similar story in the New Testament. It's found in Luke 8:22-25. Jesus said to his disciples *"Let's go to the other side of the lake."* A windstorm came, and the boat was filling with water. Maybe it was dark. Maybe they couldn't see the land. They were afraid.

Their response in their distress might seem appropriate. They cried out to God. *"Jesus, save us!"* Yet Jesus rebuked them for their unbelief. Why? Jesus had already commissioned them to cross the lake. They weren't supposed to ask Jesus to calm the storm. They were supposed to calm it!

Jesus Has Come In The Flesh

There are times to ask God to do something. The New Testament talks about prayers of petition. There are also some things we aren't supposed to ask God to do. What should we not cry out for God to do? Let's look at Matthew 10.

Matthew 10:7-8 As you go, proclaim the good news, 'The kingdom of heaven has come near.' Cure the sick, raise the dead, cleanse the lepers, cast out demons.

We aren't to ask God to do the things he's commanded us to do. We don't need to ask God to heal the sick. Peter and John didn't ask God to heal the beggar.[72] They told him to get up. We don't need to ask God to rebuke evil. He told us to rebuke it! Paul didn't ask God to rebuke the demon that possessed the slave girl.[73] He told it to get out!

As mentioned in *Present Access To Heaven,* Ephesians teaches that Jesus was raised from the dead and seated at the right hand of God, far above all power and authority! Then it says we were raised with Jesus and seated with him. We are also seated far above all power and authority. When we learn to do our part, partnering with God who is faithful to his promises, the results are marvelous!

An Antichrist Spirit Says God Controls Everything

The famous evangelist of the Second Great Awakening, Charles Finney, is called the *"Father of modern revivalism."* He often confronted the resistance of Calvinists to his evangelistic crusades. The Calvinists believed salvation and revival were up to God, so they opposed Finney's emphasis on the responsibility of the individual to repent from sin and turn to God.

On one occasion, Finney met two young men who were in anguish over the condition of their souls. They sought

---

[72] Acts 3:1-9
[73] Acts 6:16-18

7. Why Did Jesus Have To Come As A Man?

salvation, but felt no peace. Calvinists told them that since they felt no assurance of salvation, they must not be among the *"elect"* whom God had chosen for salvation. They left in despair, fearing there was nothing they could do to escape hell.

Finney assured them that if they chose to turn from sin and put their faith in Christ, they would be saved. God had done everything for them to be saved, and the only remaining responsibility was theirs. When these two men took hold of God's promise of salvation and chose to turn to the Lord, they received peace and an assurance their sins were forgiven.

This story's a great illustration of how an antichrist spirit opposes the anointing by saying everything's up to God. Few people today think about being *"born again"* in the same way these Calvinists of Finney's time did. We teach people that if they confess with their mouths Jesus is Lord and believe in their hearts God has raised him from the dead, they will be saved.[74] It's true whether they feel like it or not. We never tell anybody that if they don't feel like they are born again, it must not have been God's will to save them.

Although most people reject this deterministic attitude towards being born again, many people apply the same logic to physical healing. They think if a person is not healed, God must not have willed to heal them. Therefore, the lie that God controls everything is behind the resistance to God's work of healing the sick today, just like it was behind the resistance to people being born again in Finney's day. The lie that God controls everything denies the very reason Jesus came in the flesh, which is the authority and responsibility God gave to mankind.

The Manichean Gnostic cult called their teachers *"the elect."* They denied free will and taught determinism— the idea that everything was pre-determined; decided beforehand. For this reason some have called Calvinism the *"grandchild of Gnosticism."*

Stoicism was another Greek philosophy which influenced some of the early church fathers. Like Gnosticism,

---
[74] Romans 10:9

it taught determinism. We see the apostle Paul debating with Stoic philosophers in Acts 17:8.

Calvin took his ideas from Augustine, who had been a Manichean Gnostic before his conversion. Although Augustine rejected Manichean doctrines, he continued to hold to many aspects of their Gnostic thought. His view of man's freedom to choose departed from that of all of the early church fathers before him.

Jacob Arminius argued against Calvin's teaching. Arminius explained that *"the elect"* were those who believed and turned to Christ. Calvin taught that *"the elect"* were those whom God determined beforehand would turn to him, and thus only repented because they had been destined to repent by God. Arminius considered such a doctrine to be the teaching of the Gnostics and the Stoics. He wrote:

All the Danish Churches embrace a doctrine quote opposed to this, as is obvious from the writings of Hemmingius in his treatise on Universal Grace, in which he declares that the contest between him and his adversaries consisted in the determination of these two points: 'Do the Elect believe?' or 'Are believers the true elect?'

He considers 'those persons who maintain the former position, to hold sentiments agreeable to the doctrine of the Manichees and Stoics; and those who maintain the latter point, are in obvious agreement with Moses and the Prophets, with Christ and his Apostles.' ... The preceding views are, in brief, those I hold respecting this novel doctrine of Predestination.[75]

The charge of holding the Stoic and Manichean doctrine, which is made by some against you, is not made by them with the idea that your opinions entirely agree with that doctrine,

---

[75] Arminius, Jacobus, and John Wagner D. *Arminius Speaks: Essential Writings on Predestination, Free Will, and the Nature of God.* Eugene, Or.: Wipf & Stock, 2011. 56, 57. Print.

7. Why Did Jesus Have To Come As A Man?

but that you agree with it in this, that you say that all things are done necessarily.[76]

Calvin acknowledged the accusations against himself and Augustine that their teaching was that of the Stoic philosophers. Calvin argued that it was different because the Stoic philosophers taught nature pre-determined everything, while he believed God pre-determined everything.

We've seen that not only does the idea that *"God controls everything"* contrast with the truth revealed in the incarnation, but it can be historically traced to the influence of the Gnostics, who denied Jesus had come in the flesh. Jesse Morrel agrees:

The Early Church said that only Gnostics deny the freedom of the will; yet many denominations today say that only heretics affirm it.[77]

The truth that Jesus came in the flesh has many important implications and involves a whole system of thinking. We are examining the applications of this truth. On the other hand, a denial that Christ came in the flesh also leads to a whole system of teaching. Further study shows that the Gnostics denied everything the incarnation implies.

Many Christians say *"God is in control"* when tragedy strikes. But how far are we willing to take that logic? If a person suffers a brutal rape and murder, what does the idea that *"God is in control"* say about God's nature? I've seen far too many Christians who thought *"God is in control"* end up turning away from God, becoming angry at him, or eventually denying his existence when they suffered something painful.

If we think God controls everything, we end up with a twisted image of God. If we think he controls everything, we will see him through anything but Jesus. The Gnostics believed

---
[76] *Arminius Speaks*, Pg. 206
[77] Morrel, Jesse *The Natural Ability of Man: A Study On Free Will & Human Nature*

Jesus Has Come In The Flesh

there were two gods — an evil god and a good god. In a similar way, the belief that *"God controls everything"* leads Christians to see God as bi-polar— as if he is both good and evil.

Of course we know that in the long term, the purposes of the Lord will prevail. But God doesn't control every detail. He has given authority to mankind, and that authority can be rightly used or misused.

I have given only a short overview of how Gnosticism is related to the Calvinist version of predestination and *"God's sovereignty."* For further reading about Gnosticism, Augustine, and Calvinist doctrine, I recommend reading *The Natural Ability of Man: A Study on Free Will & Human Nature*[78] by Jesse Morrel, or reviewing www.examiningcalvinism.com

---

[78] Morrel, Jesse *The Natural Ability of Man: A Study On Free Will & Human Nature*

8. We Can Know God's Will Because Jesus Came In The Flesh

The Mystery Of God's Will Revealed In Christ

In chapter six we saw that the incarnation means God is with us. We can see God exactly as he is and know what he wants, because Jesus came as a man and God is with us. Consider the implications of this.

John 1:18 No one has ever seen God. It is God the only Son, who is close to the Father's heart, who has made him known.

We can conclude from John 1:18 that nobody can see God except through Jesus. That means before Jesus came in the flesh, nobody could clearly see exactly what God is like. The view was blurred.

Many people pray, *"God, if it be your will..."* If something happens, they assume it must have been God's will. If nothing happens, they assume it must not have been God's will. When people believe God controls everything, they think God must have permitted anything which happened, for a special purpose.

Such a mindset causes us to view God and his will through our circumstances and life experiences. If we do so, our perception of God looks different than Jesus. Yet we can only see God through Jesus. If we could see God through the events of life, Jesus would not have had to come in the flesh.

When we get our picture of God through our circumstances, we get a perverted image of God. We look at him through fallen man and the work of the devil instead of beholding him through Jesus, the sinless man and redeemer of creation.

If we think all the good and evil that happens on this earth is due to God's permission, we perceive God as having some darkness in him. We are thinking like Taoists, whose yin-yang symbol depicts the belief that there's some darkness in all light, and there's some light in all darkness. The first letter of John, written in contradiction to the Gnostics, also contradicts the yin-yang theory. Jesus' life shows us that there's no darkness in God. He's pure light, pure love, and pure goodness.

1 John 1:5 This is the message we have heard from him and proclaim to you, that God is light and in him there is no darkness at all.

If we think God controls everything, we must necessarily assume that a good God does evil so good will result. What did the apostle Paul think of such an idea?

Romans 3:8 (NIV) Why not say—as some slanderously claim that we say—"Let us do evil that good may result"?

Paul called such an idea slander! If it was slander to claim Paul said such a thing, how much more is it slander to claim God does evil so good may result? As Joseph of the Old Testament declared, God brings good out of what men meant for evil. The Lord can bring redemption in anything, but he does not will or do evil so good may result!

God always intended to reveal himself through mankind, but all men sinned and fell short of his glory. Nobody could see God exactly as he is until Jesus, the sinless man, revealed him in all of his glory.

John 14:8-9 Philip said to him, "Lord, show us the Father, and we will be satisfied." Jesus said to him, "Have I been with you all this time, Philip, and you still do not know me? Whoever

8. We Can Know God's Will Because Jesus Came In The Flesh

has seen me has seen the Father. How can you say, 'Show us the Father'?

Colossians 1:15 He (Jesus) is the image of the invisible God, the firstborn of all creation

Unless seen through Jesus, God is invisible. Because Jesus has come in the flesh, we can see God as he is. We can touch God. God is no longer far away and mysterious.

God's will is rooted in his nature. Hebrews makes it clear that God speaks to us through the revelation of his nature, and his nature is revealed to us through Christ.

Hebrews 1:1-3 Long ago God spoke to our ancestors in many and various ways by the prophets, but in these last days he has spoken to us by a Son, whom he appointed heir of all things, through whom he also created the worlds. He is the reflection of God's glory and the exact imprint of God's very being.

Do you want to know what God is saying? God's will isn't revealed through tragedies which have happened, or what people have done to you. He's not speaking through sickness and disease. Your disappointments and trials don't reveal his nature. If you could see him as he is through those things, Jesus would not have needed to come in the flesh. God has spoken through Jesus!

In the past, God spoke in various ways. God spoke in the Old Covenant, but what people could see of God through the Old Covenant was never his exact image. It was only an imperfect shadow of better things to come. It was only pointing to Christ.

Hebrews 10:1 ...the law has only a shadow of the good things to come and not the true form of these realities

Colossians 2:17 These are only a shadow of what is to come, but the substance belongs to Christ.

Jesus Has Come In The Flesh

In the last chapter, we saw that Jesus coming in the flesh was precisely what Job longed for. It was the answer to Job's prayer! Yet how many people are looking at God through Job's afflictions rather than through Jesus? If nobody can see God exactly as he is except through Jesus, nobody can see God as he is through Job. As I once heard Bill Johnson say, *"Job is the question. Jesus is the answer."* Jesus is the atonement, the mediator, the advocate, and the access to God that Job cried out for. The book of Job points to Jesus.

As we saw in chapter two, Jesus healed and delivered everyone who touched him and everyone who came to him. His will was always good, with no darkness mixed in. He revealed the Father's compassion. Jesus never told anybody *"It's not your time yet to be healed."* He never said to anybody *"My Father is allowing your affliction for a special purpose."* He never told parents *"My Father wants another angel in heaven"* when they came to him with a sick child.

Since Jesus is the express image of the invisible God, reject any view of God that doesn't look like Jesus. You can't see God as he is through anything or anyone except through Christ.

Not only can we see God exactly as he is, but we can know his will because Jesus came in the flesh. Look at what Jesus said. He came as a man and revealed to us *"everything"* the Father made known to him. He didn't hold anything back. God's will is no longer a mystery. He has made it known in Jesus!

John 15:15 I do not call you servants any longer, because the servant does not know what the master is doing; but I have called you friends, because I have made known to you everything that I have heard from my Father.

Ephesians 1:9 ...he has made known to us the mystery of his will, according to his good pleasure that he set forth in Christ

8. We Can Know God's Will Because Jesus Came In The Flesh

An Antichrist Spirit Says God's Will Is A Mystery

An antichrist spirit says we can't be sure what God's will is until time and circumstances reveal it. It denies that God's will was revealed through Jesus. Here's one of the scriptures this spirit likes to quote out of context.

1 Corinthians 2:16a "For who has known the mind of the Lord so as to instruct him?"

Many Christians quote this verse in a way that they think is exalting God. Maybe it feels like God is more magnificent and worthy of awe if he is depicted as far away, mysterious, and un-knowable. However the whole context of this scripture is about our knowing the things of God because we have been given the Spirit of God. Here's the rest of the scripture:

1 Corinthians 2:16b But we have the mind of Christ.

Jesus revealed God's will by coming in the flesh. Because an antichrist spirit denies the incarnation, it says God's will is a mystery. Don't be foolish and fall for its lies!

Ephesians 5:17 So do not be foolish, but understand what the will of the Lord is.

An Antichrist Spirit Teaches People To View God Through Anything But Jesus

God has revealed his will to us. He has put his Spirit in us because he wants to accomplish his will through us. If we forget this we will assume God must not have said *"Yes"* or decided to heal a person if we pray and nothing happens. But God has said *"Yes!"* Jesus is God's *"Yes!"*

2 Corinthians 1:20 For in him every one of God's promises is a "Yes." For this reason it is through him that we say the "Amen," to the glory of God.

Jesus Has Come In The Flesh

Everything Jesus did was the will of God, revealing the character of God. Jesus healed all who came to him. The antichrist spirit presents an image of God that's different than Jesus. How do these lies prevent Christians from demonstrating the anointing? Scripture is full of exhortations to believe, to pray with faith, to be unmovable, and to stand firm on truth.

Ephesians 6:13-14 Therefore take up the whole armor of God, so that you may be able to withstand on that evil day, and having done everything, to stand firm. Stand therefore, and fasten the belt of truth around your waist, and put on the breastplate of righteousness.

James 1:6-8 But ask in faith, never doubting, for the one who doubts is like a wave of the sea, driven and tossed by the wind; for the doubter, being double-minded and unstable in every way, must not expect to receive anything from the Lord.

If we don't know what God wants, how can we have faith? How can we stand firm? If we think whatever the current circumstances are is a reflection of God's will, we'll be double minded, driven and tossed by the wind. The antichrist spirit opposes the anointing by denying the revelation of God which we received through Jesus coming in the flesh.

Colossians 1:9-12 ...we have not ceased praying for you and asking that you may be filled with the knowledge of God's will in all spiritual wisdom and understanding, so that you may lead lives worthy of the Lord, fully pleasing to him, as you bear fruit in every good work and as you grow in the knowledge of God.

May you be made strong with all the strength that comes from his glorious power, and may you be prepared to endure everything with patience, while joyfully giving thanks to the Father, who has enabled you to share in the inheritance of the saints in the light.

8. We Can Know God's Will Because Jesus Came In The Flesh

Look at Paul's prayer above. Why did he pray that the Colossians be filled with the knowledge of God's will? So they would lead lives worthy of the Lord, bear fruit in every good work, and grow in the knowledge of God.

If we don't know God's will, we won't lead lives worthy of the Lord because we won't see him as he is in order to be able to reflect him with our lives. If we don't know God's will we won't bear fruit in every good work, because faith is impossible if we don't know what God wants. If we don't know God's will it hinders us from growing in the knowledge of God, because we do not behold him as he is through Christ.

If the church is the body of Christ, shouldn't the church look exactly like the Jesus we read about in the gospels? Why doesn't it? Because the church has not yet grown up into the full measure of the stature of Christ.

Ephesians 4:12-16 ...for building up the body of Christ, until all of us come to the unity of the faith and of the knowledge of the Son of God, to maturity, to the measure of the full stature of Christ. We must no longer be children, tossed to and fro and blown about by every wind of doctrine, by people's trickery, by their craftiness in deceitful scheming.

But speaking the truth in love, we must grow up in every way into him who is the head, into Christ, from whom the whole body, joined and knit together by every ligament with which it is equipped, as each part is working properly, promotes the body's growth in building itself up in love.

To *"attain to the whole measure of the fullness of Christ,"* we must first be convinced of God's will and of who Jesus is. We must take hold of what scripture tells us about Jesus. Then we can grow up in every way into Jesus. What does *"in every way"* mean? It includes growing in power, in love, and in purity. It includes learning to demonstrate both God's love and God's power just as Jesus did.

Jesus Has Come In The Flesh

If Jesus healed everyone and we, as the body of Christ, fail to do what Jesus did, it shows we have room to grow. Period. Instead of doubting God's will and being thrown to and fro by every wind, let's look to Jesus, the author and perfecter of our faith.[79]

Is your faith perfect yet? Have you grown up in every way into Christ, or is it possible for God's power and nature to be manifest through you to a greater degree? Of course it is! So instead of doubting who Jesus is, let's grow!

When Jesus has revealed something to be God's will, yet we don't see it, what needs to happen? First, we need to be convinced it is God's will. Then we need to *"be made strong with all the strength that comes from his glorious power,"* as we just read in Colossians 1:11. Paul said something similar in Ephesians.

Ephesians 3:16-21 I pray that, according to the riches of his glory, he may grant that you may be strengthened in your inner being with power through his Spirit, and that Christ may dwell in your hearts through faith, as you are being rooted and grounded in love. I pray that you may have the power to comprehend, with all the saints, what is the breadth and length and height and depth, and to know the love of Christ that surpasses knowledge, so that you may be filled with all the fullness of God.

Now to him who by the power at work within us is able to accomplish abundantly far more than all we can ask or imagine, to him be glory in the church and in Christ Jesus to all generations, forever and ever. Amen.

How does God accomplish his will? By revealing it to us and strengthening us in our inner beings with power through the Holy Spirit. How are we strengthened in our inner beings? We are strengthened and filled with the fullness of God as we see God as he is. By looking at him through Christ we come to know his love which surpasses knowledge. It will be evident

---

[79] Hebrews 12:2

8. We Can Know God's Will Because Jesus Came In The Flesh

that the fullness of God fills us when we do no less than what Jesus did.

God revealed his will to us when Jesus came in the flesh. He showed he wants to perform his will through us by putting the Spirit of Christ our bodies. Is this a hard teaching? Should it produce condemnation when we fail to do what Jesus did? By no means! It should be the most encouraging teaching in the world, because we know that since we have room to grow, far more is possible than what we have yet experienced.

We know God is able to do more than we could ever ask or imagine, not from somewhere up the sky if he wants to, but by his Spirit at work in us because he wants to. We are not helpless, hoping God will do something. We have the Helper, the Holy Spirit, to empower us to do what God wants.

9. The Antichrist Spirit Resists The Revelation Of Christ

Avoiding Jesus

Since an antichrist spirit opposes Christ, it will do anything possible to distract people from the revelation of Jesus. Every ungodly spirit avoids anything to do with Jesus, because salvation and deliverance come through Jesus.

As I started talking to people about the Lord and praying for them, I noticed disturbing patterns in the conversations. At first I didn't know exactly what bothered me. Then I realized a spirit opposing the revelation of Christ was influencing them. The spirit was trying to change the topic and keep them in bondage. Such a spirit can influence both Christians and non-Christians.

I learned to be assertive in such situations and not let the spirit do all the talking. Here are some common phrases people use to evade talking about Jesus. Although these might initially seem like normal things to say, experience has convinced me I'm often dealing with a spirit that's opposed to Christ.

"The Power Of Faith Is Amazing"

One night I was at the school across the street from my house. Some people were taking martial arts classes, and a girl's knee was injured. I began to talk about how God had healed me.

The martial arts instructor immediately cut me off as I was still speaking and began to talk about oriental healing arts. He did something where he pressed on the girl's knee and tried to move energy to make it feel better. It was obviously far inferior to what Christ could do, since he told me that all of them had chronic knee pain. If it really worked so well, they would all be better!

I recently visited the house of an old lady whom I'd never met before. God showed me where she had pain in her body. Every time I tried to talk to her, she cut me off. I realized it was probably a spirit trying to keep me from saying what I needed to speak. The spirit was trying to steal her attention from Jesus.

I had to be assertive. As we were leaving and everyone was saying goodbye, I interrupted loudly and said *"Wait! I have something to ask you before we leave. Do you have pain right here? And how about your right shoulder..."*

I shared three things. She had chronic pain in exactly the places I described. She had gone through surgery on her right shoulder. I laid hands on her, and the pain left. She was so happy and gave me a big hug.

The people with me immediately started talking about the *"power of faith."* One of them was a Spiritist. Spiritists believe in the supernatural, but they have many gods. It's not about Jesus. I recognized a spirit's influence when they spoke of the *"power of faith."* It was doing everything possible to divert their attention from Jesus.

Again, I was assertive, and said *"Faith is confidence, and confidence can be misplaced. This lady was healed because I have confidence in Jesus. This wasn't mind over matter, but the nature and love of God revealed. Mind over matter can never accomplish what faith in God can."* And so I began to talk about Christ.

I've had many experiences like this. In *Present Access To Heaven* I recounted a time I ministered to many New-Agers. As they were being healed, a woman advised me to release their sicknesses into a tree, so I wouldn't get sick with them. I told her I didn't have to, because Jesus already carried them.

Not long ago I received a Facebook comment on a testimony I shared, recommending a *"must read"* book about the mind's healing power. I replied that I'm not interested,

9. An Antichrist Spirit Resists The Revelation Of Christ

because *"mind over matter"* can never compare to what Jesus can do.

An antichrist spirit sometimes manifests by talking about healing or supernatural things, but taking Jesus out of the equation. The healing or testimony was meant to reveal Jesus to people, and the spirit tries to detract from that revelation by acting like it had nothing to do with Jesus.

"You Have Such An Amazing Spiritual Gift!"

I've experienced a similar scenario in the church. When a person is healed, an antichrist spirit often tries to get the attention off Jesus. Christians also sometimes talk about the *"power of faith."* Even more often, they immediately start talking about the *"spiritual gift"* of the person ministering.

The purpose of the miracle that just happened wasn't to get people to praise a *"spiritual gift"* which a supposedly *"special person"* has. It was to demonstrate what it looks like for the Spirit of God to dwell in a human being. It was to reveal God's love and compassion for a suffering person. It was to reveal Christ, who is the same in every situation, and whose Spirit dwells in every believer.

When Christians direct all the focus to a *"spiritual gift,"* I recognize a spirit at work. I am assertive. I explain how the healing demonstrates God's nature. I remind the people of Jesus' promise that all who believe in him would do the things he himself did. I tell Christians who focus on a *"spiritual gift,"* *"The same spirit of Christ dwells in you, and he wants to do the same thing through you."*

An antichrist spirit makes people uncomfortable talking about Jesus. It encourages them to talk and act in a religious way to divert attention from the revelation of Christ. The reason they're uncomfortable is often because they've been taught lies which undermine the revelation of Jesus' nature and compassion.

The healing challenges their view of Christ. It also challenges them personally. If healing is about the nature of Jesus, whose spirit dwells in Christians, they should be able to do the same things. However, an antichrist spirit has told them they can't. Focusing on a *"spiritual gift"* is a way to avoid confronting the fact that this is Jesus' nature, therefore it's what his body the church should reveal.

"What Church Do You Go To?"

Another diversion, common with unbelievers and believers, is to ask *"What church (or denomination) are you from?"* Although this may seem like a common question, I'm convinced it often comes from a spirit trying to distract people's attention from Jesus. People often ask this because an ungodly spirit makes them uncomfortable with talking about Jesus.

Other Christians may ask this question when you share testimonies with them, or when they see someone healed through your hands. It's usually because they've become comfortable with a religious, spiritualized version of Jesus. They're challenged when presented with a Christ who is the same today as the Christ of the Bible, and whose spirit dwells in Christians. They feel uncomfortable with that, and try to change the topic.

Unbelievers often ask this question as well when we tell them our testimonies and share the gospel with them. Many people would rather talk about church and religion, because Jesus makes them feel uncomfortable. A friend of mine, Judd Sands, recently made the same observation. Here are his thoughts:

One of the most common questions asked by people when they are questioned about knowing the Lord and spiritual things is, "So where do you go to church?" Or, "What religious denomination are you?"

I rarely tell them or invite them to go where I may be attending. Not because I'm ashamed to, but rather it's a diversion from the real issue. God wants to speak directly into their lives at that particular moment to set them free, and if I engage with their question it usually puts them at ease. The

9. An Antichrist Spirit Resists The Revelation Of Christ

alarm going off in their soul is making them uncomfortable as the gospel hones in on the faulty wiring that sin has caused. And they start talking about the future or a building, whatever is the way of natural thinking.

Jesus often told people to go home after he ministered to them. He knew what was in man's heart. Think about the change that would occur if a man went home to his wife and kids and said, "Guys let's get together now and talk about the Lord."

Talk About Jesus!

Maybe you've heard these phrases or similar ones before. Maybe you felt like something wasn't right, but couldn't put your finger on the problem. If so, I hope this helps you understand what's happening. It's important to recognize what's going on, because then you will know how to respond.

How do we resist an antichrist spirit? It's simple. We speak the truth to counter the lies. We don't let the spirit do all the talking through the people it's influencing. We learn to be assertive and get people's attention on Jesus. We have overcome every antichrist spirit, because Jesus lives in us.

1 John 4:4 (NIV) You, dear children, are from God and have overcome them, because the one who is in you is greater than the one who is in the world.

An Antichrist Spirit Says You Need Special Knowledge Because Jesus Isn't Enough

Like John's epistles, Paul wrote much of the book of Colossians in opposition to Gnostic teaching. The word *"Gnostic"* comes from the Greek word *"knowledge."* While the Gnostics denied that Jesus came in the flesh, they believed their *"elect"* had a special, secret knowledge, hidden to others. Instead of putting their trust in Jesus for salvation, they put their trust in this *"special"* knowledge.

Paul countered their teaching in his letter to the Colossians by focusing on everything Jesus is. He emphasized to the Christians in Colossus that everything they needed was found in Jesus. Since Paul said it so much better than I could, I've selected some of the key verses from Colossians chapter 2.

Colossians 2:2-4, 6-10, 13-19 I want their hearts to be encouraged and united in love, so that they may have all the riches of assured understanding and have the knowledge of God's mystery, that is, Christ himself, in whom are hidden all the treasures of wisdom and knowledge. I am saying this so that no one may deceive you with plausible arguments...

As you therefore have received Christ Jesus the Lord, continue to live your lives in him, rooted and built up in him and established in the faith, just as you were taught, abounding in thanksgiving.

See to it that no one takes you captive through philosophy and empty deceit, according to human tradition, according to the elemental spirits of the universe, and not according to Christ. For in him the whole fullness of deity dwells bodily, and you have come to fullness in him, who is the head of every ruler and authority...

And when you were dead in trespasses and the uncircumcision of your flesh, God made you alive together with him, when he forgave us all our trespasses, erasing the record that stood against us with its legal demands. He set this aside, nailing it to the cross. He disarmed the rulers and authorities and made a public example of them, triumphing over them in it.

Therefore do not let anyone condemn you in matters of food and drink or of observing festivals, new moons, or Sabbaths. These are only a shadow of what is to come, but the substance belongs to Christ. Do not let anyone disqualify you, insisting on self-abasement and worship of angels, dwelling on visions, puffed up without cause by a human way of thinking, and not holding fast to the head, from whom the whole body, nourished and held together by its ligaments and sinews, grows with a growth that is from God.

9. An Antichrist Spirit Resists The Revelation Of Christ

Teaching that emphasizes special, secret knowledge which is only available to a few *"elect"* is antichrist, in that it's deception meant to take people's focus off Jesus. It does so because everything people need is found in Jesus, the Christ, God's Anointed One.

If you've read the first two books of this series, you'll recall my Grandmother's vision and various experiences with angels. I welcome angels and visions from God. I often sense the presence of angels and have visions in my mind that help me minister to people. I once saw a rainbow-colored angel with my physical eyes.

These experiences glorify Jesus and encourage us to hold fast to Him. However, I have heard some Christians talk more about *"angelic encounters"* and visions than they talk about the gospel. Some of the teachings they promote go way beyond any biblical doctrine.

Are there things in the spiritual realm which the Bible doesn't tell us everything about? I'm sure there are. Nevertheless, if we seek to come to another *"spiritual level"* by searching for some secret knowledge that's not available to everyone, we are deceived.

What we really need isn't some new revelation that hasn't been made available to everyone. What we need is to understand Jesus' incarnation, death, and resurrection. We need to embrace everything these truths contain and imply. Then, we must renew our minds with them and act on them.

That is what Colossians is saying. What we need isn't something new. It's to continue with Christ in the same way we received him. Everything we need, including all the treasures of wisdom and knowledge, is found in Jesus. The Gnostics put great importance on understanding things like angelic hierarchies. Something is wrong when a person focuses more on demonology or angelology than on Jesus' incarnation, death, and resurrection.

Throughout this series, I've shared my experiences of physically sensing the glory of God. I know what has triggered

Jesus Has Come In The Flesh

these experiences. I know where the glory is. It's in the truths of Jesus' death, resurrection, and incarnation. It's in seeing God as he is by looking at Jesus.

If you want to advance your spiritual life, go back to the basic truths of the gospel. Meditate on these truths and consider how consistent your actions and speech are with them. You don't need some new, special revelation. You need to grow in the knowledge of Jesus.

I love teaching about angels. I encourage people to learn about angels and to value their ministry. It can help us to see what God is doing and partner with him. Learning what the Bible teaches about angels should lead us to focus all the more on the most glorious truths — Jesus' incarnation, death, and resurrection. Doctrines about angels should never be seen as a step beyond these fundamental truths. Rather, they point back to them.

Other Christians talk constantly about a special revelation they believe they've had of catastrophic events in the future. They major on interpretations of Bible prophesy that involve plenty of poor exegesis and speculation. Some people talk much more about a future *"antichrist"* figure, Nephilim, or aliens than they talk about Jesus!

If anyone comes to you with a *"revelation"* they think you need, test if their teaching is pointing to a greater revelation of Christ or if it's a distraction from him. Consider if their personal lives are demonstrating Jesus to people. Are they healing the sick and setting people free? Are they preaching the gospel and have fruit to show for it? Or are they puffed up with lots of talk about spiritual things but not holding fast to Christ, the head?

The apostle John, in his writing against the Gnostics, said something similar to what Paul said in Colossians. Like Paul, John warned the believers not to be led astray from the simplicity found in Christ. [80]

---

[80] 2 Corinthians 11:3

9. An Antichrist Spirit Resists The Revelation Of Christ

2 John 1:7-11 Many deceivers have gone out into the world, those who do not confess that Jesus Christ has come in the flesh; any such person is the deceiver and the antichrist! Be on your guard, so that you do not lose what we have worked for, but may receive a full reward. Everyone who does not abide in the teaching of Christ, but goes beyond it, does not have God; whoever abides in the teaching has both the Father and the Son. Do not receive into the house or welcome anyone who comes to you and does not bring this teaching; for to welcome is to participate in the evil deeds of such a person.

10. I Can Do The Things Jesus Did, Because Jesus Has Come In My Flesh
Jesus' Commission To His Disciples Extended to Us!

We read Jesus' command to his disciples to cure the sick, raise the dead, cleanse the lepers, and cast out demons. Jesus first sent out his twelve disciples to preach the gospel with these signs. Then he sent out 72 others to do the same. The last words of Jesus that Matthew records are an extension of these commands to all future disciples. A disciple of Jesus learns to do what Jesus did.

Matthew 28:18-20 And Jesus came and said to them, "All authority in heaven and on earth has been given to me. Go therefore and make disciples of all nations, baptizing them in the name of the Father and of the Son and of the Holy Spirit, and teaching them to obey everything that I have commanded you. And remember, I am with you always, to the end of the age."

Jesus' disciples were to teach all future disciples to do the same things Jesus had commanded them. The things Jesus taught his disciples to do are also commands for us. Jesus made it clear that those who believed in him would do the same things he did.

John 14:12 Very truly, I tell you, the one who believes in me will also do the works that I do and, in fact, will do greater works than these, because I am going to the Father.

How do we heal the sick, raise the dead, cleanse the lepers, and cast out demons? We can do these things in the same ways Jesus and his disciples did. Jesus most often healed people through touch. He also spoke, commanding sickness or demons to leave, commanding bodies to be whole, or commanding the person to do something. Sometimes he even did something unusual, like putting mud on a man's eyes.[81] The methods were sometimes unconventional, but Jesus had authority to do the Father's will. He passed that same authority on to us. It's up to us to use it.

As we saw in *I Will Awaken The Dawn,* the only time we read about prayer for healing in the New Testament is a referral to the story of Elijah. Elijah's prayer was combined with action and speaking in faith. He proclaimed God's word as a fact before there was a sign of anything happening.

It's not up to God to heal the sick or cast out demons. He has done his part. God put the ball in Jesus' hands, and Jesus passed it on to all who would believe in him. Don't wait for God to do the things Jesus did. He has put his Spirit in people like you, and he's waiting for you!

Part of the truth that Jesus has come in the flesh is that his Spirit dwells in us. Our bodies are his temple. An antichrist spirit denies Jesus has come in the flesh, so it denies the Spirit of Jesus dwells in believers. It denies the church is the body of Christ.

Jesus Became Like Us In Every Way

By coming as a sinless man, Jesus exemplified what's possible for any person in right relationship with God the Father. Although Jesus is God, he became like us in every way. That means he did all his works as a human being, not as God above.

Hebrews 2:14-17 Since, therefore, the children share flesh and blood, he himself likewise shared the same things, so that through death he might destroy the one who has the power of

---

[81] John 9:1-7

10. I Can Do The Things Jesus Did, Because Jesus Has Come In My Flesh

death, that is, the devil, and free those who all their lives were held in slavery by the fear of death. For it is clear that he did not come to help angels, but the descendants of Abraham. Therefore he had to become like his brothers and sisters in every respect, so that he might be a merciful and faithful high priest in the service of God.

Hebrews 4:15 (NIV) For we do not have a high priest who is unable to empathize with our weaknesses, but we have one who has been tempted in every way, just as we are—yet he did not sin.

I once heard Todd White point out that scripture says God cannot be tempted,[82] but it says Jesus was tempted. The point is that Jesus, being God, really did become like us in every way. He needed the help of his heavenly Father just as much as we do.

John 5:19 Jesus said to them, "Very truly, I tell you, the Son can do nothing on his own, but only what he sees the Father doing; for whatever the Father does, the Son does likewise.

Everything Jesus did, he did through the empowerment of the Holy Spirit. By coming in the flesh, Jesus demonstrated what's possible for any person who has been made righteous, cleansed by his blood and in right relationship with God. I know I can do what Jesus did, because Jesus came in the flesh. He became like me in every way and he did his wonders through the empowerment of the same Holy Spirit he has given me. He said if I believed in him, I would do the same works.[83] He lives in me!

If You Believe You Will See The Glory Of God

In *Present Access To Heaven* we discuss Jesus' promise that if we believe, nothing will be impossible for us. We see the only

---

[82] James 1:13
[83] John 14:12

reason Jesus ever gave for his disciples being unable to heal someone or cast out a demon was their unbelief.

Here's the story of a miracle which happened as I took hold of Jesus' promise concerning faith. I responded when the Holy Spirit reminded me of scripture, and what happened made a deep impression on my soul.

I believe this testimony will encourage you if you feel weak and helpless. I felt emotionally weak, but that didn't change the fact that Jesus lives in me. As you read, remember that I'm just sharing my experiences in growing in Christ. Jesus himself is your standard.

I'd been at a four day Christian conference which I attended annually. For some reason, I was having a really hard time at the conference. On the last night of the conference I cried loudly. I have often wept as the Holy Spirit touched me, but this was different. I felt overwhelming emotional pain, and I wasn't sure exactly why. I felt so much pain it seemed it would never end, and I didn't know how to overcome it.

Some people came to minister to me. They asked me if I'd been sexually abused. I'd never been sexually abused, but it wasn't surprising they asked. That was how loudly and desperately I was crying. They tried to counsel me, but I didn't know where the emotional pain was coming from.

I left weak; physically exhausted. The next few days were difficult. The emotional pain was overwhelming. I felt like I had no strength, but I kept holding on to life, knowing God was faithful and I had to keep going.

A few days later, I attended a service hosting Nicky Cruz. I sat in the meeting feeling exhausted and emotionally crushed, but Jesus was bigger than how I felt! I noticed a man in a wheelchair to the side of me.

As a child I read the story in Acts 3 of Peter and John meeting a lame man. Peter said *"What I have, I give you. In Jesus' name, get up and walk."* As a child and teenager, I sometimes daydreamed about doing what Peter did. I could see myself taking the hands of a man in a wheelchair and saying *"In Jesus' name, get up and walk."*

10. I Can Do The Things Jesus Did, Because Jesus Has Come In My Flesh

But the thought of doing this was terrifying! I think I even tried it before and nothing happened. Or else I was scared to be so bold and only timidly prayed for the person, with no results. Now, in my twenties, I had seen many people healed, but had never helped someone get out of a wheelchair!

Yet as I sat in that meeting, feeling depressed and weak, I couldn't stop thinking about the man in the wheelchair. As I saw him, this scripture kept running through my head again and again:

John 11:40 Jesus said to her, "Did I not tell you that if you believed, you would see the glory of God?"

In context, Jesus had commanded the stone to be removed after Lazarus died. This was his reply when Martha responded that there was a stench because Lazarus had been dead for four days. God would be glorified by a miracle, which, in that case, was the resurrection of Lazarus. In my case, I needed to believe if I wanted to see the man in a wheelchair walk.

I felt like I was at the end of my rope. I felt like I had no strength. However, I wanted to see God glorified by the man in the wheelchair walking. It was scary. I could imagine the embarrassment of doing something so bold in a public place and nothing happening. Yet, I didn't care anymore. If I believed, I would see God's glory. I wanted to see this. The scripture kept replaying in my mind.

At the end of the meeting I walked up to the guy and said *"What's your name?"* He attempted to reply, stuttering slowly, *"I-I-I-I d-d-don't know."*

I had never before in my life seen such an expression of extreme frustration on the face of a human being. His condition was worse than I had realized! It seemed quite severe. Even so, I wanted to see the glory of God. So I asked, *"Do you want to get out of that wheelchair?"*

He could barely respond but managed to nod his head *"Yes."*

I said loudly, *"Then, in Jesus' name, get up and walk."*

Jesus Has Come In The Flesh

Every head around us turned. I was in the spotlight and it felt like my heart was in my throat. If this didn't work, I was going to look so stupid. But if I believed, I would see God's glory.

He hesitated, afraid. I said, *"Come on, I'll help you,"* and I took his hands. He got up and walked, with great difficulty at first. As he began to walk, I started yelling, *"In Jesus name, strength come into his legs now! In Jesus' name, everything be whole now!"*

It seemed every step was a little stronger. He walked about 15 feet with me holding his hands and sat down again, tired, but radiant! Just as before it seemed I had never seen such an expression of frustration, it now seemed like I had never seen such joy on the face of a human being. His family was gathered around, ecstatic. They kept thanking me again and again.

I couldn't sleep all night. I still felt emotionally weak and tired, but the scenario of what happened kept playing through my mind. I kept seeing the picture, etched on my mind's eye, of the joy on the man's face after he walked. Although this happened about eight years ago, I often cry when I tell the story. The emotional impact was that great.

The next day after work I went to the evening meeting again and talked to the man and his family some more. They told me he was a heavy equipment operator, but he had a stroke and the doctors didn't know if he would ever walk again. He longed to recover and return to his job.

This wasn't an instant miracle of being 100% better in a moment. Even then, it was remarkable. I try to report what happens as accurately as possible. Knowing the fear of the Lord, I speak with sincerity, openly stating the truth and persuading men, as Paul did.[84] Even though this was not the most dramatic miracle I have seen, it was one of the most emotionally charged ones.

Skeptics might point out that he still left in a wheelchair that night. He was also sitting the next day. However, I was able to have quite a conversation with him. Although he still

---

[84] 2 Corinthians 5:11

10. I Can Do The Things Jesus Did, Because Jesus Has Come In My Flesh

had some difficulties with speech, it was a huge difference in comparison to the night before! He could communicate. Remember, he had been unable to even tell me his own name the previous night, and could barely speak at all. It was remarkable he could speak so well now and had walked, taking into account his condition the previous evening.

He and his family were elated, now expecting recovery. This was a huge deal. The weight of the doctor's words, that he might never walk again, was no longer pressing on them. Although I lost contact with the family (by misplacing the email address), I believe he continued on to full recovery.

Spiritual things are foolishness to the earthly minded.[85] The earthly-minded person says *"Look, he's still not completely better."* Yet the earthly-minded response foolishly ignores what has been manifest of God's work. The book of Romans says when people don't give thanks, their foolish hearts are darkened. [86]

If we are spiritually minded, we're like Elijah, who as soon as he saw a little cloud coming out of the sea, cried out *"It's going to rain."*[87] We thank God and rejoice for what's about to happen even before we see it happen. We stand firm[88] rejoicing, until the full manifestation. We lay our hands on the sick and they will recover.[89] It's a fact.

This story also reminds me of my grandmother's recovery after a near death experience. As I lay hands on her and God's power touched her head, she immediately spoke words she'd lost the ability to say. Full recovery wasn't immediate. Significant improvement came immediately, and recovery continued after that.

This experience of ministering healing to a stroke victim helped me grow in my confidence in the Lord. I can't explain why I had felt such emotional pain, that I would cry the

---

[85] 1 Corinthians 2:14
[86] Romans 1:21
[87] 1 Kings 18:44
[88] Ephesians 6:13
[89] Mark 16:18

way I did. I don't understand why it was such a difficult time for me. However, I do know God will never leave me or forsake me.[90] His promises are true, and they don't depend on how I feel.

How I feel doesn't change the truth about God's faithfulness. What I feel doesn't change the fact that the Holy Spirit dwells in me and is ready to help people around me. Though you feel weak, God, who has given you his Spirit, is strong. May this encourage you that no matter what you feel emotionally, God's promises are true.

Because Jesus became like us in every way, he had nothing we don't have. He was subject to the same weaknesses as we are. We have the same Holy Spirit he had. Therefore, nothing should limit us that didn't limit him. Jesus is the firstborn among many brothers,[91] and we are his brothers. He isn't ashamed to call us brothers.[92] We've received the same glory Jesus received from the Father,[93] and the Father loves us just as he loves Jesus.[94] We have everything he had.

Frustration And Making Healing Too Complicated

When I became convinced of God's will to heal people and started laying hands on them, I saw many wonderful healings. However, sometimes I felt frustrated because of healings I wanted to see, but didn't. It especially hurt when I opened up my heart to minister to people facing life-threatening diseases and saw little change. It's hard to explain the emotional pain I've faced at times because of that frustration.

Once at McDonalds I commanded a friend's eyes to be perfect so she wouldn't need her thick glasses. Her eyes began to go in and out of focus, as if the knob on a pair of binoculars was being turned back and forth. Every time, they came more

---

[90] Hebrews 13:5
[91] Romans 8:29
[92] Hebrews 2:11
[93] John 17:22
[94] John 17:23

10. I Can Do The Things Jesus Did, Because Jesus Has Come In My Flesh

into focus until she was healed of nearsightedness and didn't need glasses! However, a few days later she felt something funny in her eyes and put her glasses back on. When she did that, her eyes completely regressed!

I know this may seem a little thing to get down about, but for me it felt like the straw that broke the camel's back. I got very discouraged because of this and I didn't see another miracle happen for a whole month. When people are healed it often feels like strength and love are exploding from my heart. However, when I got discouraged, I tried to lay hands on people but I felt tired inside. I needed my heart to be strengthened and refreshed by the Holy Spirit.

Even when I felt discouraged, I couldn't stop going, because I knew what I had seen was real. Stopping because of what wasn't happening didn't make sense, because many people were still being healed! Again and again the Holy Spirit strengthened me and lifted me when I felt discouraged, and more miracles kept happening.

Because of the frustration over some people not being healed, I researched healing even more. I listened to different teachers and read books about healing. I studied everything I could about specific *"spiritual roots"* of various diseases. I learned about *"removing hindrances to healing"* by leading people in repentance from any sin that might be related to the problem, asking if they had any unforgiveness that needed to be dealt with, and breaking *"generational curses."*

I was confused about many things. I didn't read in scripture of Jesus having counseling sessions with people to get them healed, but it seemed a lot of experienced people were having more success by doing these things. I also read promises of scripture like this:

Mark 11:23 "Truly I tell you, if you say to this mountain, 'Be taken up and thrown into the sea,' and if you do not doubt in your heart, but believe that what you say will come to pass, it will be done for you."

If this scripture was true, I should be able to speak to the mountain no matter what anyone else thought, and it would move. Jesus didn't say *"If you speak to the mountain and get the other people around you to believe with you, it will be done for you."*

On the other hand, I read in Matthew 13 that even Jesus was only able to do a few miracles in Nazareth because of their unbelief. Why did Jesus so often encourage people to believe? Why in Mark 5 did he put everyone out of the house before he raised the girl from the dead? I'd been taught he was getting all the unbelief out.

Although I knew I needed to understand something better, I generally thought *"The more faith, the better."* I thought if I had really strong faith, maybe it could overcome the unbelief of others. Yet it still seemed the unbelief of others could hinder me from demonstrating God's power. That was frustrating, especially in situations where it felt like everyone was against me.

I was mostly ministering to Christians. I often told them how I became convinced it was God's will to heal everybody. Then I did things like leading them through visualizing Jesus on the cross carrying their sickness, or leading them in prayers of forgiveness. I especially did such things when somebody wasn't healed the first time. I figured I needed to get any hindrances to healing out of the way. Some people were healed like this, yet something bothered me.

I did minister to unbelievers once in a while, but not much. I was more timid about it. I saw in scripture that healing miracles were a sign for unbelievers, in order to lead them to salvation. If healing miracles were supposed to lead unbelieving people to repentance and faith in Christ, it didn't make sense that I should need to get them to repent or believe before the miracle could happen! The way I had learned to minister healing made it difficult to minister to unbelievers.

I knew very well I should never tell anybody *"You weren't healed because of your unbelief."* I was there to encourage people, not put blame and discouragement on them.

10. I Can Do The Things Jesus Did, Because Jesus Has Come In My Flesh

Yet because I thought the unbelief of others could dull the effectiveness of my faith, it was hard to not feel frustrated with people when they showed unbelief. Even though I never told anyone it was their fault they weren't healed, it was all too easy to wonder if maybe a person wasn't healed because they still hadn't forgiven somebody or repented from some sin.

I even felt angry sometimes when I heard a person say something expressing unbelief. Yet many of these people had never seen a miracle before and had little reason to believe — in contrast to Jesus' disciples, who had already seen great miracles and even healed many sick people themselves, but still showed unbelief.

By the emphasis on dealing with *"hindrances to healing,"* I thought as if people had to jump through hoops to be healed. This kind of thinking didn't produce grace in my heart towards people. It only hindered me and my effectiveness in ministering to others.

Meeting Dan Mohler

Dan Mohler is a popular teacher, with sermons on You Tube. Many people have become familiar with his teaching through the *Schools of Power and Love*. I met him about a year before *Power and Love Ministries* was established.

A couple in my church told me about Dan, an assistant pastor at a church in the adjacent county. They knew how much I spoke of healing so they thought I'd be interested in meeting him. They told me Dan held meetings at a country firehouse somewhere between Lancaster and Reading, PA. I lived in Lancaster, and it was a forty-minute drive away. The meetings were on Thursday nights, if I remember correctly. I decided I had to go.

I had never before heard anybody speak like Dan did! It was clear to me that he was genuine and he lived what he taught. Dan spoke about God's promises and the simplicity found in Christ.

Jesus Has Come In The Flesh

2 Corinthians 11:3 (KJV) But I fear, lest by any means, as the serpent beguiled Eve through his subtilty, so your minds should be corrupted from the simplicity that is in Christ.

Dan talked about how God spoke to Adam and Eve, and Satan added a *"Yeah, but..."* to what God had spoken. Jesus said in scripture that believers will lay hands on the sick, and they will recover.[95] Jesus said if we believed, nothing would be impossible for us.[96] Jesus said if we spoke to the mountain to be cast into the sea, not doubting but believing, it would surely be done.[97]

In scripture, Jesus gave only one reason for his disciples not being able to heal somebody: their unbelief. They had already healed many sick people and cast out many demons, returning with rejoicing.[98] Yet when they couldn't get a young boy free, Jesus said it was because of their unbelief.[99]

Instead of holding to the simplicity of Christ's promise that if we believed, nothing would be impossible for us, we had added all kinds of other conditions. *"Yeah, but..."* Then we ended up doing all kinds of things scripture never speaks of Jesus doing when he ministered to people, and saying all kinds of things Jesus never said.

The responsibility was on the believers to heal the sick, and not on the sick to believe and get everything right so they could be healed. If God's goodness brings people to repentance,[100] why did we require people to repent before they experience the Lord's goodness by being healed?

Dan shared some amazing testimonies which illustrated the truths he taught. One of them was the story of an alcoholic woman with stage four cancer, which I shared in chapter four. The lady was healed long before she let go of unforgiveness,

---

[95] Mark 16:16-18
[96] Mark 9:22-24
[97] Mark 11:23
[98] Luke chapters 9 and 10
[99] Matthew 17:20
[100] Romans 2:4

10. I Can Do The Things Jesus Did, Because Jesus Has Come In My Flesh

stopped blaming God, and stopped drinking. She only repented when she realized God had healed her!

Hearing Dan speak made me cry. He talked about the very things that had confused me, but I still had questions. After the meeting I drilled Dan, asking him *"What about Jesus not being able to do miracles in his hometown because of their unbelief?"* and other questions. I wasn't questioning him because I opposed what he said. Rather, I wanted to believe what he believed. If I was going to believe it, I wanted to be fully convinced. Dan answered all my questions with a big happy smile!

Why Did Jesus Only Heal A Few People At Nazareth? Why Did He Put Everyone Out Before Raising A Girl From The Dead?

Why did Jesus only heal a few people at Nazareth? Why did he put everyone out before raising a girl from the dead? These were two of the questions I asked Dan. Maybe the answers will help you as much as they helped me.

We read of Jesus' rejection at Nazareth in Matthew 13:54-58 and Mark 6:1-6. Matthew says Jesus didn't do many deeds of power there because of their unbelief. Mark says Jesus couldn't do any deed of power there, except for laying his hands on a few sick people and curing them. Jesus was amazed at their unbelief. So I asked Dan, *"Why couldn't Jesus do many miracles in Nazareth?"*

Dan's answer was simple, but I'd never even considered it. Jesus wasn't laying his hands on the sick in Nazareth and saying *"It's not working guys. You have too much unbelief, and it's hindering me."* Can you imagine that? Rather, few people in Nazareth came to Jesus to be healed. Even so, the people who Jesus did lay hands on were healed.

This made a lot of sense to me, because scripture tells us of people in other regions thronging Jesus, bringing all the sick to wherever he was, laying them on the ground, and

Jesus Has Come In The Flesh

begging to touch even his cloak.[101] Contrast this with Nazareth, where the people were filled with rage and tried to shove Jesus off a cliff.[102] You don't get much chance to lay your hands on many people when they're trying to shove you off a cliff, do you?

Dan pointed out several places in scripture where Jesus did healing miracles in the face of hostility and unbelief. He healed a man with a withered hand when those watching were so hard-hearted they were just seeking a reason to accuse him.[103] The Gospel of John makes it clear that Jesus confronted such unbelief that even *after* he did so many miracles among them, they still didn't believe!

John 12:37 (NIV) Even after Jesus had performed so many signs in their presence, they still would not believe in him.

If they still didn't believe even after Jesus had done many miracles, an *"atmosphere of unbelief"* surely didn't stop Jesus from doing any miracles! This question was well-answered. My other question was, *"Why did Jesus have to put almost everybody out of the house before he raised a girl from the dead?"*[104]

That question had a simple answer too. They were making a lot of noise. They were an annoyance and a distraction. Nothing in the text says Jesus needed to *"get the unbelief out of the house"* in order for God's power to work.

Many people have read that into the text, but it doesn't say that. This scripture doesn't contradict the promise Jesus gave, that nothing would be impossible for us if we would believe. Jesus didn't say *"If enough people believe to create an atmosphere of faith, nothing will be impossible."* Neither did he say *"If you lay hands on the sick and they believe they will recover."*

---

[101] Matthew 14:35-36, Luke 4:40, Mark 6:54-56
[102] Luke 4:28-29
[103] Mark 3:1-6
[104] Mark 5:39-43

10. I Can Do The Things Jesus Did, Because Jesus Has Come In My Flesh

Dan completely convinced me. I no longer felt confused. If I believed, nothing would be impossible for me. Yes, people are sometimes healed when they forgive someone, repent of sin, or receive emotional healing, and these things are good! However, I stopped making them conditions a person needed to meet to be healed. I no longer saw things like sin and the unbelief of others as *"hindrances to healing."* There was one biblical condition— that I believe.

What Happened When I Simplified Things?

When I ministered to someone and nothing happened at first, I no longer tried to find all kinds of things that might *"hinder"* the healing. I no longer needed to do a counseling session or convince the recipient to believe more. I would simply stand firm.

Things were so much easier this way! My strength was renewed, and I finally began to see unbelievers healed. I now had the faith to approach them. I saw many more miracles than before, because I didn't let go of my faith so easily by wondering if the recipient had unforgiveness, a hindering sin they didn't repent of, or too much unbelief. People's words of unbelief stopped bothering me so much.

Soon after I met Dan, I went on a trip to visit my good friends at *The Son Spot* in Ocean City, Maryland. On that trip I continued challenging myself to reach unbelievers with God's power. Here are two of the miracles which happened. I would never have had faith for these before my change in thinking.

I had the chance to go around with a brother who was delivering food from the ministry's food bank to families in need. He told me this would be a good opportunity for some people to be healed, since I liked to minister healing.

Before we visited one particular family, he told me about some of the lady's spiritual problems and her alcoholism. Previously, I would have thought *"I'll tell her Jesus carried her sins and sicknesses. I'll encourage her to repent and ask God to help her stop drinking, and then when she receives forgiveness she can receive her healing."* Now, I thought *"God will heal her and the demonstration of God's goodness through the healing will give her opportunity and grace to repent."*

Romans 2:4 (KJV) ...not knowing that the goodness of God leadeth thee to repentance?

When we met the lady, I asked her if she had any need of healing. She showed me her swollen legs and feet. I told her *"God will heal your legs, and he will also help you get free from alcoholism."* As I spoke with her, the Lord showed me her kidneys and her heart also needed to be healed. When I asked her about this, she was stunned and told me about her kidney and heart problems. It was the kidney problem that caused the water retention in her feet.

I told her *"God's going to heal your kidneys and your heart to show you his goodness, and this will be an opportunity for you to get free from addiction."* I prayed for her and commanded her body to be healed. She felt heat on her kidneys, and then she looked at her feet and said *"Look, they're shrinking."*

When she said that, they started to shrink really quickly. She screamed and ran over to her husband who was sitting in an easy chair, smoking and watching TV. She started yelling, *"Look, my feet are shrinking, look!"* He didn't seem so excited, but the swelling disappeared before our eyes.

This lady's physical issues were caused by her sin—which she had not repented of. She also admitted to having lots of anger and bitterness. The last I heard, she still hadn't gotten her life right, even after she was healed. However, this didn't stop the Holy Spirit from touching her and drawing her with his goodness.

Another time on that same trip, as I walked back to *The Son Spot,* the Holy Spirit showed me somebody had a right knee injury which needed healing. Then I saw some women on the street and realized one of them was limping. It looked like

10. I Can Do The Things Jesus Did, Because Jesus Has Come In My Flesh

they'd been partying and drinking. At least one of her friends was drunk.

I approached them and asked if it was her knee that was causing her to limp. It was. They looked weirded out, and uncomfortable that I was talking to them. I pointed my hand and said *"In Jesus' name, knee be healed right now."*

When I said that, her whole face changed and became contorted with a look of hatred and rage. Have you ever been cussed out by someone who didn't want to hear about Jesus? It looked like a long string of profanity was about to come out of her mouth. But before she said anything, I said quickly, *"Just wait. Does your knee hurt now?"*

She looked confused and said *"No."* I said *"Move it and see if it hurts."* She did. No pain. Still confused, she walked around and bent it more, and I asked again, *"Does it hurt at all?"* She said *"No."* After three or four rounds of this, she finally realized it was really better. I said *"Well, I'm glad your knee is better,"* and I walked away. Her whole countenance changed, softened. She said *"Thank you."*

Here was a woman who thought she hated Jesus and hated Christians. She thought she hated Jesus, but she really just didn't know him. She was probably bitter about past experiences with religion. It looked like she was about to cuss me out. None of that stopped God's power from touching her.

Those are only two of the stories I remember of what happened after I received God's correction through Dan's teaching. There are many more.

I began to believe for the lungs of smokers to be cleared out and for the livers of alcoholics to be made new. I also laid hands on people who had sexually transmitted hepatitis. These people were sick as a direct result of their sin, yet I was proclaiming God's mercy to them.

Smokers felt their breathing get easier and their lungs clearing. I remember one man who had abused alcohol and had cirrhosis of the liver. I held my hand behind his back and said *"In Jesus' name, liver be whole! Toxins leave!"* He physically felt something like a vacuum in his body sucking toxins out of his liver. Instead of repentance being a requirement to get healed, the healing was God's call to repentance for these people if they had not yet repented.

One young guy suffered an injury playing soccer. He felt God's power and got better when I laid my hands on him, commanding the injury to be healed. Even though it wasn't 100% better that night, it convinced him the healing I talked about so much was real. I found out from others that he previously mocked me for always asking people if they needed healing. Even skeptics and mockers can be healed!

New Agers and Spiritists were healed as well. When I asked if anybody at a picnic table needed to be healed, one man said *"Do I have to believe what you believe for this to work?"* I said *"No, what happens is based on what I believe, not on what you believe."* He did not accept what I believed about Jesus, but he said they would give me a chance to try to get them healed if they didn't have to believe what I do for it to work. About 20 people were healed, and most or all of them had New Age beliefs.

My life changed in a major way after Dan convinced me to simplify things. The events which happened and their underlying truths led me to a greater understanding of God's nature and love. Having an expanded revelation of God's nature also made me love him more. Some of the miracles made me cry. I saw that God is full of mercy. God is willing to pour out his goodness even on people who hate him. Jesus told us to love our enemies, because God loves his enemies. He isn't holding men's sins against them.[105]

Matthew 5:43-45 (NKJV) "You have heard that it was said, 'Love your neighbor and hate your enemy.' But I tell you, love your enemies and pray for those who persecute you, that you may be children of your Father in heaven. He causes his sun to rise on the evil and the good, and sends rain on the righteous and the unrighteous.

---

[105] 2 Corinthians 5:19

10. I Can Do The Things Jesus Did, Because Jesus Has Come In My Flesh

God's kindness to those who made themselves his enemies impressed me. Seeing this stopped me from being bothered so much when people opposed me. Even if people mocked me, it couldn't stop me from loving them.

Nothing That Didn't Limit Jesus Should Limit Us

You've probably heard stories of physical healing occurring when a person forgave someone, repented of sin, or received *"inner healing."* Maybe you have experienced this. We certainly have basis to understand that many physical issues are often caused by spiritual or emotional problems. We saw how closely physical health is connected to our spiritual state in chapters two and three of this book.

Like physical healing, inner healing and repentance are also the work of the Holy Spirit! Physical healing can happen in conjunction with inner healing or releasing forgiveness. The Holy Spirit may lead us to challenge a person to turn from sin or to forgive someone they bitterly resent. Yet I no longer believe we should view a person's unbelief, sin, or unforgiveness as *"blocks"* we need to deal with before God can physically heal them. Why?

Jesus didn't need to take people through counseling sessions to physically heal them. Everyone who touched him was healed. When did Jesus leave people sick because they hadn't yet worked through their emotional or spiritual issues? If these things didn't hinder Jesus, they shouldn't hinder us. We can find so many reasons why we think it's *"not working"* that we let go of faith instead of standing firm.

In my experience, many people have received emotional healing through the physical healing that God accomplished. I've seen people who were numb with emotional pain and felt like God didn't love them, weeping after they were physically healed. Physical healing reveals God's nature to people, healing hearts and empowering them to forgive others. Many people, like the alcoholic lady with cancer in Dan's story, have come to repentance after being physically healed by the Lord.

God wants to touch people's hearts and their bodies as well. Either one can happen through the other. People may receive physical healing as the Lord touches their souls or as they forgive others or turn from sin. On the other hand, they may first be physically healed and then respond by repenting and forgiving others. Emotional healing may come through the physical healing or vice-versa. Neither one is contingent on the other.

Don't let the problems you see in a person's heart and soul destroy your faith for their physical healing, because the physical healing will reveal God's goodness to them so as to lead them to repentance. Yes, God often touches people's bodies as soul issues are dealt with. Just don't make repentance, forgiveness, or dealing with emotional issues hoops people must jump through before they can be healed.

Don't imagine these things are blocking God's power to heal physical bodies. They didn't stop Jesus! Jesus healed all who came to him. When the church grows up in all things into the full measure of the stature of Christ,[106] the only thing people will need to do to be healed is to come to us.

---

[106] Ephesians 4:12-16

11. The Antichrist Spirit Denies Christ Lives in You

You've Already Overcome All Antichrists, If Jesus Lives In You!

We've studied some of the most important aspects of the incarnation and learned to recognize the lies of an antichrist spirit. We've seen that an antichrist spirit opposes the anointing, and his lies keep the church from walking in the anointing.

Not only do I know the truths I've written about from scripture, but I know them from experience by putting them into practice. Miracles increased in my life as I recognized antichrist lies. I never saw a single person healed through my hands until I learned to see God through Jesus and not through my circumstances. But since then, I've seen many miracles.

We must recognize and reject the lies an antichrist spirit whispers in our ears, freeing our minds from its lies. We must also be assertive in the face of external opposition from an antichrist spirit, both through unbelievers and through believers influenced by a spirit denying the incarnation. Whether an antichrist spirit is whispering its lies to us or speaking through someone else, we tell it to shut up and then we do the talking and proclaim Christ has come in the flesh.

Remember that if Christ lives in you, you've already overcome all antichrists.[107] Overcoming opposition is a matter of recognizing and rejecting the lies, telling the spirit to shut up, and countering its lies with truth.

---

[107] 1 John 4:4

Confronting Excruciating Pain And Much More

I went through a period of about a year where I progressively grew to understand what it means that Jesus came in the flesh. During that time, I took a trip out of state with my family.

We visited a man who was suffering greatly. He had constant pain for many years. One of his legs was amputated due to diabetes. His skin was covered with sores and he had multiple physical problems. He was also living in sexual sin. A great deal of mental torment and emotional pain was apparent, along with all the physical problems.

As we talked with him he said *"God must have a reason for me to suffer like this."* My heart was stirred! I spoke to him about seeing God through Jesus. I said, *"Jesus is the same today, and it's God's will to heal you now, but God works by putting his Spirit in men. The problem is that the body of Christ, the church, needs to grow and become convinced of who Jesus is. If God's will is done through me right now, you will be healed."*

He said *"Pray for me!"* My sister and I, with hearts full of fire, rebuked the pain and the disease. *"Be healed now, in Jesus' name!"*

Shut Up You Lying Spirit!

After spending considerable time laying hands on him and commanding healing, little changed. The pain level was the same. The only thing he noticed was that his vision improved slightly. I felt my heart drop in my chest. Disappointment. We got his hopes up, and then we let him down. I knew it was Jesus' will to heal him, but we weren't able to demonstrate what I knew in my heart to be true. At least that was what I felt.

Then a thought came to me. The Bible says I can do what Jesus did, because Jesus lives in me. I had just begun to realize that the Spirit of Christ dwelling in Christians is an extension of the truth that Jesus has come in the flesh. Therefore a spirit that denied I could do what Jesus did was a spirit that denied Jesus had come in the flesh. It was antichrist!

11. The Antichrist Spirit Denies Christ Lives In You

I didn't say a word out loud, but my heart shouted. *"Shut up, you lying antichrist spirit! You're saying Jesus doesn't live in me and I can't do what Jesus did. But you're a liar! This man will be healed, and Jesus will be glorified in this situation!"* I was aggressive, strengthened in my innermost being by the power of the Holy Spirit, bursting with strength. I refused to be disappointed. I stood on truth, saying *"Shut up!"* to the devil.

Four days later I got a phone call from the man. The pain had been the same when we said goodbye to him, but by the end of the day it was gone. Years of chronic, excruciating pain, not a moment without pain— gone! Within four days, all of the sores on his body had cleared up.

Maybe sometimes you feel like you can't do what Jesus did. It doesn't matter what you feel. It's a lie. If Jesus lives in you, you can do the same works as he did and even greater works. Step out and start doing them, no matter how you feel. Never back down!

This story is about exercising the power and authority that Jesus demonstrated, but the same principle applies to loving like Jesus did. An antichrist spirit says you can't love like Jesus did. It says that person in your life is too difficult, or too evil. It says you can't forgive the person who wronged you.

An antichrist spirit says your spouse is testing your patience way too much and you can't treat them like you know Jesus would. It says you can't demonstrate Jesus' wonderful character to everyone around you— because he was Jesus and you're not. It denies that Jesus lives in you.

We must do the same thing in these situations as I did when that lying spirit told me I couldn't help the sick man. We respond, *"Shut up, you lying antichrist spirit! Jesus lives in me, and I can love like he loves! I can forgive like he forgives! Jesus lives in me, and his nature will be manifest through me. His love will be demonstrated through my life!"*

Dealing With Spiritual Opposition To The Message

One of the sections in chapter seven was *When Not To Cry Out To God*. We mentioned Moses' prayer and Jesus crossing the stormy sea with his disciples. This was a message I preached a few months ago to a small group of Christians here in Brazil. I encountered opposition after the message from a spirit which denied Jesus had come in the flesh.

I had three words of knowledge to share with this small group. They were physical problems for which people there had need of healing. For the first two, I knew who the individual was who had the problem. For the third one I saw a vision in my mind of intestinal polyps, but I wasn't sure who had the condition.

As I finished my message, a man was already standing up front beside me to speak! He interrupted me before I could share the words of knowledge! It was as if everything I just said had gone in one ear and out the other. He went on and on about crying out to God to split the water when we are in front of a Red Sea. Then he began to pray, asking God to rebuke the devil!

The whole message had been about us exercising authority and doing what Jesus told us to do, because God gave us the Spirit of Christ to empower us. I had just talked about God's rebuke to Moses and Jesus' rebuke to his disciples when they asked God to do that which he commanded them to do.

Yet this man went on and on speaking as if everything was up to God and as if Jesus never had come in the flesh. You might think what he did was incredibly rude. It was! But he didn't intend to be rude by interrupting me. I don't think he even realized he was saying anything different than what I had just said. I believe he actually thought he was agreeing with me!

I have experienced this repeatedly. It's the influence of a spirit opposed to God's work which has a stronghold in a person's mind. The person is unable to hear or understand us when we talk about the Spirit of Christ dwelling in believers.

11. The Antichrist Spirit Denies Christ Lives In You

Such people interrupt and pray loudly, begging God to do something and going on and on so nobody has a chance to rebuke the sickness or oppressing spirit.

Another time, recently, I had just shared some testimonies and begun to lay hands on people. Miracles were happening. A lady began praying loudly *"God, we know that you can heal these people in your way and in your time..."* She went on and on, praying as if Jesus had never come in the flesh; as if God was far from us and we couldn't know his will! It was extremely disruptive. The time was that moment, and the people were already being healed!

People who do this in church settings are usually nice and devout. They are well-meaning and don't realize what they are doing, but a spirit is influencing their minds. It speaks lies and will do anything to take all the attention and disrupt what the Holy Spirit is doing. When people are so unaware of what they are doing and so unable to hear what we are saying, a spirit is influencing them.

Be As Gracious As Possible, But Be Assertive!

If you are healing the sick, some of you may have similar experiences to what I have described. The person interrupting probably doesn't even realize what they just did. Don't take offence! I have learned to be as gracious as I can, but to be assertive. I encourage you to do the same. We get afraid of interrupting or of being rude ourselves. However, sometimes you have to interrupt, as graciously as possible!

Once God gave a woman a dream telling her she needed to talk with me. This was so I could lead her into being born again. Yet, when she came, everyone else was talking so much I didn't share with her. I didn't want to interrupt anyone. She left. However, I made a point of finding her again before I left that city, and she did give her life to the Lord!

When the man interrupted me as I finished preaching, before I could share the words of knowledge, I had to take charge of the situation and interrupt him. I tried to do it in the most gracious way possible. If I hadn't interrupted, he would have gone on and on until the meeting ended and everyone was leaving. I wouldn't have had the chance to speak and an antichrist spirit would have done the rest of the talking through him.

I shared the words of knowledge. I asked the first two people if they had pain in certain places. They did, and they were healed. The first one had already experienced a decrease to about half the pain level before I even prayed for her. The second was completely pain-free after hearing the word of knowledge, so she didn't need more prayer. I also described my vision of intestinal polyps.

Guess who the third word of knowledge was for? It was for the man who interrupted me! Of course, his condition was not immediately testable like the others were, but I believe he was healed as well. Although he didn't stop begging God to rebuke the devil, I am confident some of the other people there got it! They were excited and encouraged by the message.

Dealing With Disruptive Prayers

Sometimes we face opposition through disruptive prayers. Disruptive prayers are prayers that people pray as if Jesus never came in the flesh and as if the gospel were not true. A spirit that denies Jesus has come in the flesh uses such prayers to try to do all the talking and oppose what the Holy Spirit wants to do.

The opposition we face from the devil is basically in the form of lies exalting themselves against the knowledge of God. God never gave authority on the earth to Satan, but to men. Satan needs to deceive men and get them to agree with him to accomplish anything. God also works through men. The incarnation demonstrates this truth. Jesus came as a human being, and his Spirit dwells in people who have been born-again.

When other people are influenced by an ungodly spirit's lies, they may be unable to hear the truth. They may be disruptive, or do anything possible to change the topic. In these situations, we must be assertive. We don't take offense at the

11. The Antichrist Spirit Denies Christ Lives In You

person, but we realize this is the influence of a lying spirit. Here's another recent experience of dealing with disruptive prayers.

I laid hands on a man after church a few months ago. The pain left and he was healed. He got excited after feeling God's power. Another person also needed healing, so I encouraged him and a few others to minister to her. I taught them the importance of commanding the person's body to be healed, because we know God's will and know that Christ in us is the hope of glory.[108]

The guy started to pray a long prayer, asking God *"please heal this woman."* I stopped him and asked how she was doing. No difference. I encouraged him to do it again, but this time to command *"In Jesus' name, pain go and back be healed."* Even then, he seemed unable to bring himself to speak to the condition with authority in Jesus' name, as opposed to begging God to heal her. Why? He was still thinking as if Jesus didn't dwell in him, as if he had no authority, and as if he couldn't do what Jesus did. He was listening to the lies of a spirit that denied the incarnation.

Then the man's wife came and joined the prayer. She went on and on, begging God to do something, saying *"God, we know that you can heal this woman."* I'm sure she didn't realize how disruptive it was. She would have prayed all night if someone didn't stop her.

I had to do something. I had to be assertive. If I didn't interrupt, she would have gone on praying until everyone was anxious to leave as soon as they could get away. The lady sitting in the chair, who needed to be healed, would probably have gone home discouraged and in pain.

I interrupted the long, repetitive prayer and asked the lady receiving ministry if she felt any difference. She didn't. She was discouraged, about to get up and leave. I said *"Wait, don't worry! You will be healed. In Jesus' name, all pain get out. Be healed now."* I asked her how it was. Better. I did the

---

[108] Colossians 1:27

same thing again, and all the pain was gone in about one minute.

What Was Happening?

Praying seems like a *"spiritual activity."* However, a spirit that denies Jesus' incarnation has influenced the prayers, thinking, and actions of many Christians. When we pray as if God is far away and his will is mysterious, we are praying as if Jesus never came in the flesh; and that is a prayer of unbelief. When we act as if the Spirit of Christ doesn't dwell in us; as if everything is up to God and we have no part in it, we are acting as if Jesus never came in the flesh.

As we saw in *I Will Awaken The Dawn,* the prayer of faith is a prayer of thanksgiving. The prayer of faith is certain of the Father's will. The prayer of faith is also combined with action. If we pray as if Jesus never came in the flesh, we will spend a lot of time in religious activity with few results. We will spiritualize everything until there's little tangible fruit to our faith.

I'm not into lots of religious activity with little to show for it. I've had too much of it, and I don't have time for it. I remember when I used to go to a different church service almost every night. I went to seek the Lord, but little happened. I spent too many years acting and thinking as if God were far away. I want to see something happen— now. I want to see Jesus glorified. I want everyone to know he's not just a nice story. He's tangible. We can touch God, because Jesus came in the flesh.

We've all agreed with an antichrist spirit's lies at one time or another. It's not that we don't acknowledge Jesus has come in the flesh. It's that we sometimes act and speak as if he hasn't. Even though I've broken free from so much of the antichrist mindset, I still recognize when an antichrist spirit is lying to me and I need to tell it to shut up.

12. God's Dwelling Place

An Anti-Christ Spirit Says A Building Is God's House But Denies Your Body Is His Temple

Under the Old Covenant, God commanded people to make various animal sacrifices. Hebrews speaks of these things as a shadow of better things to come, and not the true form of the realities.

Hebrews 10:1 Since the law has only a shadow of the good things to come and not the true form of these realities, it can never, by the same sacrifices that are continually offered year after year, make perfect those who approach.

Much of the book of Hebrews reveals the completion and fulfillment of prophetic images of the Old Covenant. According to Hebrews, the objects and functioning of that old system were only imperfect *"sketches"*[109] and shadows of better, heavenly realities. When the heavenly realities of the New Covenant came, the old shadows become obsolete and soon disappeared.[110]

What would be the purpose of making animal sacrifices today, since Christ has come? To do so would be an affront to the message of the gospel. Animal sacrifices pointed to Christ, and now that Christ has shed his blood there's no longer any place for animal sacrifices.

---

[109] Hebrews 8:5, 9:23
[110] Hebrews 8:13. They became obsolete when Jesus inaugurated the New Covenant by his death, and disappeared when the temple was finally destroyed in A.D. 70, as Jesus said it would be.

Jesus Has Come In The Flesh

In the same way, a building housed the presence of God under the Old Covenant. Yet that temple was only an imperfect sketch of the incarnation. It pointed to the Spirit of God dwelling in man. Look at what Jesus said:

John 2:19-22 Jesus answered them, "Destroy this temple, and in three days I will raise it up." The Jews then said, "This temple has been under construction for forty-six years, and will you raise it up in three days?" But he was speaking of the temple of his body. After he was raised from the dead, his disciples remembered that he had said this; and they believed the scripture and the word that Jesus had spoken.

Jesus had just finished driving out the animals and flipping the tables of the money changers in the physical temple. The Jews thought Jesus spoke of the physical temple, but he spoke of his body. This was the perfect reality of which the physical temple was only an imperfect type and shadow.

We are the body of Christ and the temple of God. He has made his home in us! Jesus prophesied the destruction of the temple built with human hands.

Mark 13:1-2 As he came out of the temple, one of his disciples said to him, "Look, Teacher, what large stones and what large buildings!" Then Jesus asked him, "Do you see these great buildings? Not one stone will be left here upon another; all will be thrown down."

Stephen, before being martyred, and Paul, speaking in Athens, said the same thing. God doesn't live in houses made with human hands. No building is the house of God.

Acts 7:48 Yet the Most High does not dwell in houses made with human hands

11. The Antichrist Spirit Denies Christ Lives In You

Acts 17:24 The God who made the world and everything in it, he who is Lord of heaven and earth, does not live in shrines made by human hands

Just as offering animal sacrifices today denies the sacrifice of Jesus' body, calling a building *"God's house"* denies the incarnation. Animal sacrifices were only an imperfect shadow of the true reality to come, Jesus' sacrifice. To offer them would be to act as if Jesus never shed his blood for us.

In the same way, the temple of the Old Testament was only an imperfect shadow of the incarnation, the Spirit of God dwelling in the temples of human bodies. To treat a building as God's temple now is to act as if Jesus never came in the flesh.

God's doesn't live in houses made with human hands! We don't go to the house of the Lord. We arc the house of the Lord! If we have buildings, their purpose must be to serve people, who have become the true temple of God.

I see so many Christians who think they *"go to the house of the Lord"* to meet God, yet they act and speak as if they don't know the Spirit of Christ lives in them. Much talk of *"going to the house of the Lord"* is often combined with speaking as if God were distant, as if his will were a mystery, and as if his spirit did not dwell in his body, the church.

Putting the focus on a building as *"the house of God"* is another way an antichrist spirit tries to disrupt and do all the talking, through the people it's influencing. We respond by being assertive and pointing the focus back to the truth that God has put his Spirit in us.

I recently heard a pastor preaching a whole sermon on getting God's presence to come to the church building by our sacrifices. Didn't God already get his presence into us (if we have received him) through the sacrifice of Jesus? I don't need to go anywhere to meet God. His presence goes everywhere I go!

This same pastor regularly preaches as if Jesus never came in the flesh. He speaks as if God controls everything, as

Jesus Has Come In The Flesh

if God's will is a mystery, and as if God is inaccessible. Does he himself deny Jesus came in the flesh? No.

He doesn't deny the incarnation, but he denies much of what it implies. He himself is not antichrist, but an antichrist spirit influences him. If a person denies one implication of the incarnation, they tend to deny its other implications as well. I'm not saying this pastor is unsaved, but an ungodly spirit manifests in his preaching.

Of course, I encourage meeting regularly with other Christians. As Ephesians says, the body of Christ builds itself up in love.[111] We meet to encourage each other and build each other up. However, no building is God's house! Whether a home or an auditorium, buildings are only tools to serve us. Their only value is in serving people.

I became involved with a small Baptist church in Brazil about three years ago. It was a place with a pure spirit, with sincere love, and better teaching than many other churches in the area. The teaching was uplifting for the most part, as opposed to a lot of harmful teaching in some of the other churches.

Yet, they didn't have a building of their own at that time. They met in a school, and then at people's houses. I heard someone say it *"wasn't a real church"* because it didn't have a building. However, the word for *"church"* in scripture doesn't have anything to do with a building. It's an assembly of people.

One friend, Steve Hill, shares the story of visiting Armenia after an earthquake. Homes were destroyed and people homeless all around.

...A second story is from an Armenian city which suffered terribly from the Armenian earthquake of December 7, 1988 which killed at least 25,000 people across that country. On visiting this city I was told that an area of the center was still rubble from the earthquake and that people living in the rubble

---

[111] Ephesians 4:16

11. The Antichrist Spirit Denies Christ Lives In You

suffered even to the point of rats gnawing on their little children.

In driving around the town I was shown a brand new Armenian Apostolic Church (their state church) of impressive stone which cost 2.8 million dollars where the candles and icons slept warm and dry at night. We also came to a brand new Armenian Evangelical Church with rooms for computer labs and English classes. It too was a beautiful stone building. I was told it cost 4 million dollars to build and the computers and hymnbooks slept warm and dry at night.

We then had a meal with a couple with five children plus grandma living in a two bedroom apartment along with another brother, his wife and their baby. They were asking for help since the brother had no work and could not afford his own place. I asked if this brother was looking for work and was told that he had been working on the construction of the new, independent, charismatic church in town.

This was a church where the who's who of the charismatic world came to speak. So I asked why he was not still working there and was told that he had not been able to continue since his weekly pay had not even covered the cost of his bus fare to get to work. The fact that a church would not pay a poor man a living wage made me angry.

Then that afternoon we were driving to another appointment and my host said that we would drive past the church under construction. It was a very impressive building with three story white stone columns across the front. My mind was trying to take in the obvious wealth contrasted with the oppression of the poor who were building this idol temple when I glanced to the other side of the street and my jaw dropped.

Across the street was a full city block of rubble left over from the earthquake of twenty years ago. People who slept wet and cold in the rubble while rats attacked their kids woke up every morning and looked out at the Christians building a palace to house their pride.[112]

---

[112] Hill, Stephen and Marilyn. *The Luke 10 Manual.* Nashville Tennessee: Broad & Holman, 1996 (FAQ of chapter 9)

Because God has chosen human bodies as his temple, our top priority must be to serve people. An antichrist spirit would have people serve a building. In Steve's story above, the so-called *"house of God"* took precedence over caring for the true temples God has chosen— human beings. I've experienced similar scenarios in a western context. If we have buildings, they must serve people. May we never get our priorities so twisted that people are serving a building!

Keep Swinging The Hammer!

We have explored many of the ways an antichrist spirit manifests itself in religious settings. As you've read this book, I'm sure you have recognized ways you've confronted an anti-Christ spirit's lies, whether personally or through others.

How do we break the hold of these lies in religious settings? I've seen positive change in the mindsets of people around me. It's important to remember that when people are influenced by a spirit, they often do not realize what they are doing. If people are disruptive, don't be offended personally. Be patient and gentle with people, but don't let the spirit do all the talking through them. Speak truth!

Being assertive can be difficult because we don't want to offend people, but people don't always get angry when we speak truth. I've often been able to be assertive, even interrupting, without causing offence. If people do get offended, continue to speak the truth with humility and grace. The Holy Spirit can help you to do so!

I remember helping build a hurricane shelter in Belize, Central America. We were carving a place out of solid rock to build a septic tank. I worked with a pick and sledgehammer. It was tough work! I could hit the rock a few times in the same place with the sledge, and it wouldn't break much visibly. However, the structure of the rock was being weakened with each blow. After enough blows, the whole area I was hitting started to crumble.

11. The Antichrist Spirit Denies Christ Lives In You

Jeremiah 23:29 Is not my word like fire, says the Lord, and like a hammer that breaks a rock in pieces?

Remember that God's word is like a hammer which breaks up the rock. Keep swinging the hammer. Keep speaking God's word. Keep loving people, even when they interrupt you. Don't be discouraged when it seems like what you say goes in one ear and out the other. Don't stop because it looks like nothing has cracked yet. It can take perseverance to change deeply ingrained religious mindsets which cloud people's thinking.

I felt the same resistance when I lived in the US. The Lord helped me to be assertive, yet gracious, in the spirit of love. With perseverance, I saw many people begin to *"get it."* I saw Christians break out of mindsets that hinder the church from partnering with the Holy Spirit. I saw others begin to do wonders in Jesus' name. Now I'm in Brazil. I expect the same.

Walking In The Anointing

I was once frustrated with many years of powerlessness. I believed God did miracles, but I wasn't sure it was always his will to heal. I thought there might be exceptions. Once I broke free from the influence of an antichrist spirit, miracles happened all around me. Wherever the church lacks power, the influence of an antichrist spirit can be found.

If Jesus lives in you, you have already overcome all antichrists. The anointing is the Spirit of Jesus within you. Walking in the anointing is a matter of recognizing and rejecting the lies of an antichrist spirit. Then, you begin to think and act according to the truth that Jesus has come in the flesh.

Have you seen that if we reject one implication of the incarnation, we tend to reject the others as well?

If we don't understand that God gave authority to men, we will think God controls everything.

If we think God controls everything, we will look at him through the events of life and not through Jesus.

If we look at God through the events of life and not through Jesus, we will believe God's will is a mystery.

Jesus Has Come In The Flesh

If we think God's will is a mystery, we will relate to him as if he is far away.

If we believe he is far away, we won't think according to the truth that he has put his Spirit in our bodies individually and that the church is his body corporately.

If we don't understand that our bodies are God's temple, we will call a building *"the house of God."*

If we don't realize the Spirit of Christ dwells in us, we will believe the lie that we can't do what Jesus did.

If we think God controls everything, seeing God through life experiences instead of through Jesus, we will reject the scriptural promises of healing in the atonement.

If we reject the promises of healing in the atonement, we embrace the Gnostic dichotomy between the body and the spirit.

If we embrace a false dichotomy between the body and the spirit, the gospel becomes spiritualized, theoretical but not tangible.

When that happens, we undermine faith in Christ's atonement for forgiveness and deliverance from sin. We lose our effectiveness.

An antichrist spirit can only keep Christians from manifesting Christ by getting them to believe its lies. You've seen the lies now. Reject them. Behold the glory of God in the face of Jesus, become like Jesus, and show the world what Jesus looks like. Go and demonstrate with power, love, compassion, and purity that Jesus has come in the flesh. Make the world around you like heaven!

Appendix: Jesus Come in the Flesh Vs. The Lies of an Antichrist Spirit

Jesus Has Come in the Flesh	Lies Of An Antichrist Spirit
The physical body is a holy and valuable part of the human being. The Spirit of God dwells in human bodies. Jesus came with a physical body.	The spirit is holy and good but the physical body is evil. The body and spirit are disconnected, because one is bad and the other is good.
Jesus suffered physically and carried not only our sins, but our physical pains and sicknesses on the cross.	Since the body and spirit are disconnected, you can believe in spiritual salvation but it doesn't apply to the body.
Jesus went around healing the sick primarily because of his compassion. He healed people because people, and their bodies, are valuable to God.	Jesus' primary motive in healing the sick was to prove he was God. What God really cares about is your soul, not your body.
God chose human bodies as his temple. Since our bodies are holy, we are to honor God with our bodies. Sexual sin is sin against our own bodies. Jesus rose from the dead with a physical body, and we can also expect a bodily resurrection.	Your body is bad, so sex is evil. Physical pleasures and joys are bad. Or Your body is evil and your spirit is good, so it doesn't matter what you do with your body. It's disconnected from your spirit. Your body's not eternal anyways.
Jesus is the image of the invisible God. The only way to clearly see the Father is to look at Jesus.	Since God is in control, we can see him through our experiences and disappointments, even if the picture we get looks a lot different than Jesus.

Jesus fully revealed the Father's will to us by coming in the flesh. Jesus made known to us the mystery of God's will.	God's will is a mystery. Whatever will be will be. We can't be sure what God wants to do until we see what happens.
Jesus came as a man because God gave authority to man and chose to accomplish his will on earth by co-laboring with men. God needed a righteous man. God is still looking for righteous men, cleansed by the blood of Jesus and filled with the Holy Spirit. The church is the body of Christ.	God doesn't need you. You don't have anything to do with whether God's will gets accomplished or not. God controls everything.
Jesus is Immanuel, "God with us." We can touch God because Jesus came in the flesh.	God is far away, distant, mysterious, un-knowable, and in-tangible.
Scripture teaches not only that Jesus came in the flesh, but that he has come in our flesh. The Holy Spirit dwells in us who believe, and it is "Christ in us" who is the hope of glory. He works through us.	Your only hope of glory is God somewhere up there in the sky. If he wants to do something he will do it from heaven. You can only hope that he might answer your begging prayers. He doesn't need you to do anything. Far be it from you to be presumptuous about what he wants!

You can do all the works Jesus did, and greater works. You have the same Holy Spirit as he. Jesus was subject to every weakness that we are, yet without sin. He, like you, was powerless on his own and fully dependent on the Spirit of God which dwelt in his human body. He was made like us in every way.	You can't do what Jesus did! He did his miracles as an all-powerful God. You could never be like him.
The church is the body of Christ. Our bodies are temples of the Holy Spirit. We can't "go to the house of the Lord" because we are the house of the Lord. The temples in the old covenant were symbolic shadows of the "better things" that have come with Christ — the Spirit of God dwelling in man. God does not dwell in temples made by human hands. If we have buildings, they are to serve men, whose bodies God has chosen as his temple.	It's wonderful to "go to the house of the Lord." You need to take care of your church building because it is God's house. You need to behave in an extra-special way when you "go to the house of the Lord," because you meet God in that building.
Jesus is the only way to the Father. Faith is confidence in Jesus. The exercise of spiritual gifts is meant to reveal the Spirit of Christ in the church. Spiritual gifts demonstrate what it looks like for the Spirit of God to dwell in man, and they demonstrate what any man with the Spirit of God can do.	"The Power of Faith" is amazing. Faith is mind-over-matter. You don't really need Jesus for it to work. It works without him too. Spiritual gifts are cool because some people are really gifted with special talents!

About The Author

Jonathan Brenneman was born in Rochester, New York and raised in Pennsylvania. Although a very troubled child he was at the same time very religious. He read the Bible from cover to cover when he was seven years old, all the while questioning and wondering about the existence of God.

When Jonathan was nine years old, he woke up one morning with bad back pain. His mother prayed for him, and to his surprise, he felt something like a hot ball of energy rolling up and down inside his back, and the pain melted away. It was shocking to say the least, but it convinced him God did exist! He later told his friends, "I know that God is real. I felt his hand on my back."

In spite of this experience, Jonathan still had no peace. He prayed the "sinner's prayer" but with no change until two years later when he had a "born again" experience. It felt like heaven opened and unexplainable joy and peace descended upon him! He was different, and knew it! The things he had felt so guilty about that he tried unsuccessfully to change, were simply gone.

After this time, Jonathan dedicated his life to the Lord as a missionary, going on his first mission trip at age fourteen. As a teenager and young adult he continued to travel and learn languages. Then, in a time of desperation when he was twenty years old, Jonathan went to a Christian conference where the Lord touched and encouraged him. It was the start of a supernatural lifestyle and growing in spiritual gifts, during which time many amazing miracles and healings began to happen.

Jonathan worked in construction, but in between jobs he began to visit churches in the United States and Canada as well as in Latin America and Eastern Europe. His ministry journeys have included Russia, Ukraine, Poland, Italy, Canada, Mexico, Belize, and Brazil. In these places Jonathan has encouraged the believers and shared testimonies, and spoken with unbelievers and prayed for them. He's also worked with children and seniors. He's dedicated a lot of time to talking with, praying for, and encouraging people wherever he goes, all the while growing in the experience of a love for people that's beyond understanding—for it is God's love. Jonathan believes it's a wonderful and tremendous privilege to be able to serve the people for whom Jesus gave his life.

Jonathan is now a missionary in Rio de Janeiro Brazil with his wife Elizabeth, and daughter Rebekah. He loves people, enjoys being with them, and rejoices at seeing what the Holy Spirit does in their lives. He likes to minister in the role of teaching, laying hands on the sick, visiting the elderly, and working with children—always loving them so they in turn will learn to love others with the love of God.

Contact

You can get in touch with Jonathan through his blog at www.gotoheavennow.com, at Goodreads, or through his Facebook author page, *Jonathan Brenneman*.

Amazon reviews are the author's tip jar! They also help to get the message out to more people. If you have enjoyed this book, please consider leaving a review on Goodreads and/or Amazon.com.

Also By Jonathan Brenneman

Of The "Heaven Now" Series
Part 1: Present Access To Heaven

Present Access to Heaven presents a strong scriptural foundation for Christians to experience heaven while on earth, regardless of earthly circumstances. This book expounds on the unspeakably glorious riches that are available to every believer. It deals with subtle mindsets which undermine the truth of the gospel and hinder us from living fully in the reality accessible through Christ.

Because the truths shared may seem *"too good to be true,"* *Present Access to Heaven* is filled with true stories, illustrating that these are not just theories but real possibilities for every believer. This book is loaded with encouragement and will challenge you to come into an experiential knowledge of the Lord's goodness as never before!

JONATHAN BRENNEMAN

PRESENT ACCESS TO HEAVEN

HEAVEN NOW SERIES PART 1

Part 2: I Will Awaken the Dawn

I Will Awaken the Dawn builds on the scriptural foundation laid in *Present Access to Heaven*. Learn from both scriptural insight and testimonies how to *"Awaken the Dawn"* of the knowledge of the glory of the Lord, with praise, thanksgiving, and declaration.

No matter how dark and impossible your surroundings may seem, they become heaven to you if your eyes are opened to see the Lord there. When you see that you are in heaven because you are in God's presence, heaven will begin to manifest around you. The earth is presently full of the glory of the Lord, but it will also be filled with the knowledge of the glory of the Lord, as the waters cover the seas!

I WILL AWAKEN THE DAWN

HEAVEN NOW SERIES PART 2

JONATHAN BRENNEMAN

Other Books By Jonathan Brenneman

I Am Persuaded
Christian Leadership As Taught By Jesus

Jonathan Brenneman in his *I Am Persuaded* provokes, jabs and challenges our sacred cows of church leadership. Yet, the jabs are not hurtful because they come from Scripture. This is not a reactionary book filled with leader bashing but a graceful and excellent presentation of mostly forgotten principles concerning how Jesus and the early church taught and practiced leadership.

All the key and at times controversial words are discussed: rule, obey, submission, apostles, authority, and spiritual covering. Excellent exegesis on these words is provided and is foundational to the author's conclusions. If you find yourself disagreeing, then, by all means, do a better exegesis. I think that will be difficult. Jonathan Brenneman has personally made a paradigm shift in his life and shares it with us. Will you?

I Am Persuaded is more than a fine Bible study, it is filled with real life stories which illustrate servant leadership. It is well written, fast paced, and provokes fresh thinking. I believe the reader and the church will be healthier when these principles are put into practice. Will you be persuaded? Will you undergo a paradigm shift? Read and find out. This is a good book and its message needs to be heard.

DR. STAN NEWTON—*Missionary in Bulgaria;*
Author: Glorious Kingdom.

I AM
PERSUADED
Christian Leadership as Taught by Jesus

JONATHAN BRENNEMAN

The Power-And-Love Sandwich

Why You Should Seek God's Face AND His Hand

If you've started to step out in the supernatural things of God, it's likely that may have found yourself on the receiving end of a great deal of opposition. While you may have anticipated that those closest to you would be supportive and encouraging, instead your testimonies may have been met with a backlash. Fellow believers may have suggested that your focus on spiritual gifts is unbalanced. It may have been said that you're too preoccupied with signs and wonders.

In Jonathan Brenneman's book *The Power And Love Sandwich*, he explores the theological position of seeking God's face in conjunction with seeking His hand. Jonathan puts things into perspective and helps us to see through scripture that we don't have to pick one or the other. Both are liberally and unapologetically available to us. We can simultaneously embrace both the power of God and the love of God without having to forego one to embrace the other.

This book is a must read for those who intend to move in the power and love of God. You will learn to confidently walk in both the fruit of the Spirit as well as the gifts of the Spirit. The misguided objections of well-intended believers won't have the same power to break your spirit. Instead you will learn to shake it off, love them despite their opposition and remain kingdom focused.

***CHERYL FRITZ**—Founder*
Inside Out Training and Equipping School

THE POWER & LOVE SANDWICH

Why You Should Seek Gods Face AND His Hand

Jonathan Breneman

Made in the USA
Middletown, DE
17 February 2023